The outcast Joseph

Rachel Velasquez

The Outcast Joseph

The story of the unwanted, unloved,

and discarded.

However, not forgotten!

Rachel Velasquez

Rachel Velasquez

Release of Second Edition

by

Seven Daughters of OM Publishing

Copyright © 2022

ISBN: 978-1-957815-00-8

Dedication

I dedicate this book to all the *Josephs* of the world.

To all the dreamers who know there is more!

You are a precious child of the

Most High Elohim / EL ELYON. עֶלְיוֹן

Rachel Velasquez

Acknowledgements

A special thank you to my husband, Hervey.
He has been patient as I sit and write.
He has never complained about my writing,
which is sometimes, day and night. He has supported
me in more ways than I care to share at this time.

Thank you, Yah, for my husband, Hervey.
Watch over him as we continue to walk with You.

I am even more grateful to my
Lord and Savior for giving me the love of writing.
Ruach Haqodesh inspires my stories.
I am honored to be writing what Yahuah/Yahweh
puts on my heart and imagination.

Book cover artwork by Merav Nakash and Marteau

Reference to Names of God

From the Strong's Concordance.

EL – H410 - God

ELYON – H5945 - Most High

ELOHIM – H430 - God in plural form, the Godhead-Father, Son, and Holy Spirit

YHVH – H3068 - are the Hebrew letters English style, but people pronounce it Yahweh or Jehovah. I have learned that Yähüäh or Yähōvéh is the more proper pronunciation. I use YAH for the short name YH or yud hey.

RUACH HAQODESH – H7307 and H6944 – Holy Spirit

ADONAI – H136 - Lord

KADOSH or QODESH – H6944 - Holy

ADONAI ELOHIM TZ'VA'OT – H136 H430 H6635 – Lord God of hosts

HAYAH HAYAH – H1961 – I AM THAT I AM

EL SHADDAI – H410 H7706 – God Almighty

Yähüshüäh or YAHUSHA – H3068 H3467 – meaning YHVH is salvation, most say Jesus

YESHUA or Yëshüä – H3091 – meaning YHVH is salvation

HAMASHIACH – H4899 – The Messiah

HaBara / CREATOR – H1254 – bara is the Hebrew

Rachel Velasquez

Table of Contents

Psalms 77:11

I will remember the deeds of YHVH;
Yes, I will remember Your wonders of old.

Psalms 139:8-10

If I ascend to heaven, You are there;
If I make my bed in Sheol (the nether world, the
place of the dead), behold, You are there.
If I take the wings of the dawn,
If I dwell in the remotest part of the sea,
Even there Your hand will lead me,
And Your right hand will take hold of me.

Chapter 1 First Class

Joseph sat looking out of his first-class seat, headed home after a long trip to Europe. He had recently made some changes that had taken his life in a completely different direction than he would have ever thought possible. Joseph saw how his entire life had been so difficult, lonely, and prophetic. He closed his eyes, and his life started to replay in his mind.

After a few weeks of life, a loving couple had adopted Joseph. Growing up, all he knew about his biological parents was that his mother was possibly a teenager who had not been able to keep him. However, he grew up knowing his adoptive parents as very loving and caring in his early childhood. Joseph's earliest memory was when he was four years old. Both of his parents worked outside of the home, and he was at the daycare giver's house. He was playing in the front yard when a dog came into the yard and attacked him. Joseph was on his tricycle. He heard barking, and suddenly the dog was dragging him. The trauma and pain seemed to return. His heart was pounding, and it almost felt as if it would come out of his chest. Joseph opened his eyes for a moment.

His next memory was of the car accident at age seven as he closed his eyes. His family was going on a camping trip. The car ahead of them was pulling a trailer. The trailer came loose and forced their car off the road. His dad attempted to avoid the trailer, but he lost control of the vehicle; it rolled over. He could hear the ambulance, everything was upside down, and he felt squashed. He heard his dad's voice asking, "Joseph, are you okay? Joseph?" His father's voice echoed in his ears. He lost his mom that day. He opened his eyes again and felt the sadness of not having grown up with his mom. He missed her loving arms and tenderness. Joseph could almost smell her perfume.

Joseph asked the flight attendant for a glass of water. He closed his eyes again. Joseph's next memory of being a victim of bullying throughout his school years felt like it had just happened.   It did not matter what class or school he was in; bullies always found him. Joseph had tried to lay low or become invisible, but he could not hide. He had been called every name in the book, punched, flushed, and his homework was stolen. Avoidance and becoming invisible did not work, so he decided to defend himself. That ended badly too. Joseph experienced a suspension for fighting in middle school. His father put the fear of God in him if he ever fought again. Seeing his father's angry face forced him to open his eyes again.

Joseph's next memory was the one that left him utterly alone in this world. He was a freshman in high school when his dad died of a broken heart. His dad missed his wife so much and always blamed himself for her death. He had become a heavy drinker. It was hard to say if he was a full-blown alcoholic, but he always smelled of alcohol. Joseph could smell alcohol. He opened his eyes, and the young man next to him was drinking.

Joseph closed his eyes again and remembered his father's funeral; few people attended. His dad had alienated most of his family and friends. His uncle William was crying. He spoke, "Joseph, you are welcome to stay with me. I know your dad pushed everyone away. Would you like to come and stay with me?" He knew that he did not have many choices. Joseph understood this most likely meant another school change.

Suddenly the man next to Joseph began to speak. "Hi, my name is Timothy. May I share a story with you?" Joseph answered, "Please do not think of me as rude, but I would prefer not to speak. I have a few things on my mind." Timothy continued, "You see, my mom died yesterday, so I am on my way back home for the funeral." Joseph interrupted, "Sir, I would rather not discuss your mother." Timothy was not listening or hearing him, "She was a great mom. She loved everyone. I was her favorite child, but I walked away from the family life and never returned. That was about twelve years ago. I did not even bother to call her. She never gave up on me. My mom called me all the time and left messages. I just never returned her calls." Joseph felt a little irritated and turned to face Timothy, "So you had a mom who loved you, and you left? My mom died when I was seven. I did not get to grow up with her. You need to forgive yourself. Ask God to forgive you. The Bible tells us to honor our mother and father. She is no longer here, but you can ask her to forgive you. At least you will have spoken those words. I am sorry for your loss."

Timothy asked, "How do you know there is a God?" Joseph sometimes questioned this, too, because of his life. He thought, 'YAH, how do I answer this?' After a moment, Joseph replied, "I have had my doubts at times too. I look at my life and wonder why. I know I am not worthy. Although, I see God all around me. Can you imagine; what Jesus must have suffered for us? I am a miracle just being here today." Timothy looked confused, "What do you mean?" Joseph smiled, "I haven't introduced myself. My name is Joseph. Please accept my apology for being unfriendly and rude." Timothy answered, "I didn't even notice. What do you mean you're a miracle?" Joseph answered, "You wouldn't believe me if I told you." Timothy said, "Try me. I need to get my head off my mother's death and how worthless I am, according to all my siblings."

Joseph laughed, "Alright, but you asked for it." He felt a sense of peace come over him at the thought of sharing his story.

Joseph thought to himself, 'I have never told anyone about my Life which makes this the first time I will be sharing it. I hope I can get through it.' He looked at Timothy and started his story, "My biological mother abandoned me at childbirth. I was left in a dumpster. When the sanitation workers came to dump it, one of the men said he felt like he was supposed to look inside. He had never done anything like that before, so he felt weird. He said he almost did not look. This city employee had gotten a feeling of urgency to look inside. He saw a varsity athlete's jacket at the bottom and saw it move. He thought it must be a rat but felt he had to reach in and grab it. When he lifted the jacket, I fell out."

3

Timothy almost shouted, "No way, dude!" Joseph nodded his head. "I was thrown away like trash. Unwanted, unloved, rejected, and abandoned. They immediately called the ambulance and police to the scene. I heard the story goes something like this."

Joseph paused for a moment, "They rushed me to a nearby hospital, where I remained in the hospital for several weeks. Due to my weight of three pounds and one ounce, they say I was born about six weeks too early." Timothy interjected, "Did they find your real mom?" Joseph shook his head, "No, they didn't. My adoptive parents had been attempting to adopt for years when I happened into this world and into their arms. My mom had been a volunteer at the hospital. I heard that my mom was so happy when she got the word that I was coming home with her. You could say she felt that God answered her prayers, and I was a gift from heaven."

Timothy interrupted, "Dude, you make me feel worse, not better. Are you telling me that I took heaven away from my mom?" Joseph asked, "Is that what your spirit is saying?" Timothy asked, "What do you mean, my spirit?" Joseph continued, "Some call it your conscience. We are flesh, soul, and spirit. The Bible says that we are created in God's image, and He is Spirit." Timothy answered, "I guess then my spirit says yes. I can't even imagine how lonely my mom must have felt when I never reached out to her. It was hard for me because I never wanted to hear her sadness, let alone see her sad."

Joseph asked, "Do you believe that when we die, that's it?" Timothy responded, "No. I believe in heaven; I guess I just didn't put the two together. I guess I lost faith over the years." Joseph reassured him, "I can see how it can happen to people. It happened in my life too. When I was seven, my mom died in a car accident, so I didn't get to experience motherly love for very long." Timothy spoke, "My mom showed us so much, love. She provided everything I needed; I never felt lonely because she was so full of life. But unfortunately, I felt so guilty that it was better not to keep in touch with my family. I never wanted to hear her voice because I knew I had broken her heart. I guess I've been a fool all this time. I didn't appreciate my mom. Now it's too late."

Joseph smiled, "No need to feel guilt or shame. Instead, ask the Lord for forgiveness. He forgives all our sins. He is a very loving Father." Joseph continued, "Would you like to pray?" Timothy answered, "No, man. I'm not ready and not worthy."

Joseph was in deep thought about his mom. He didn't have too many memories of her, which bothered him. Finally, after a few minutes of silence, Timothy spoke. "Please continue with your story. I didn't mean to interrupt. Sometimes I speak before thinking."

Joseph smiled and, after a few moments, continued. "I don't know that I really remember my mom, but I always had pictures of her that I used to look at. For example, I had a picture of her and myself when I was about two years old; she seemed happy. My mom was wearing this white dress with polka dots; a glow emanated from her. I remember her eyes were bright and full of life. Her smile always lit up a room. At least, that was what dad always said." Thinking about the picture made Joseph miss his mom. He continued, "Every time I looked at that picture, I missed her."

He glanced at Timothy and smiled. "What was your mom like?" Timothy smiled, "Mom was funny. She had a great sense of humor and would always tease us and make us giggle. My mom was also full of life. I remember that the room lit up just by her being in it. She didn't even have to speak; her presence made it glow. I remember one time; I'm not sure how old I was when she made a celebration cake. When my dad went to cut into it, it was a brick, which she had frosted to make it look like a cake. We all laughed so hard. Dad just laughed. The way he looked at her, I knew he loved her maybe more than life. She had made a real cake and hidden it in the pantry. That was a fun night. I do have a lot of great memories of her."

Joseph was quiet, then added, "That's what you want to remember. Focus on all the good memories and don't focus on mistakes because it's too late to correct them. Maybe if we could go back in time, we could change things, but we need to move forward since we can't. Right now, you need to focus on being a brother to your siblings. Is your dad alive?"

Timothy shook his head. "No, he passed away when I was in college. You would have thought that would have been a good reason to come back, but my mom seemed sad. I hated seeing her sad." Joseph continued, "Listen, this is a problem, and if you deal with it before you arrive, you will have a clear conscience. I'm not a pastor or priest, but I can help you pray." Timothy shook his head again, "I don't deserve to feel any better after all the pain I caused my mom." Joseph interjected, "None of us deserve it, but Jesus made a way so we can have freedom. It's a simple prayer. Lord, forgive me for the pain I caused my mom." He watched Timothy, but there was no reaction. Timothy was in deep thought.

Joseph picked up his book with the pretense of reading, but his thoughts were back on his mom. He closed his eyes, and he had another memory. 'It was his birthday party, and his mom had made his cake into the shape of his favorite car. It looked just like his toy car. It was blue with the number five on the door.' Suddenly he heard the airline flight attendant asking Timothy, "Would you like something to drink?" Joseph opened his eyes and smiled. She was a beautiful woman with a smile that brightened the plane. Timothy ordered a black coffee. "May I please have a glass of water?" Joseph didn't feel like anything else, but Lucy asked, "Would either of you like anything else? We will be serving dinner in a couple of hours." Timothy answered, "No." Joseph smiled, "No, thank you. I will wait for dinner."

Joseph smiled to himself, deep in thought, 'Lucy reminds me of my high school sweetheart Cyndy.' Then he heard Timothy, "She is beautiful. I see that you noticed her?" Joseph chuckled, "She reminds me of someone I once knew. She was a sweet girl." Timothy pressed, "Sounds like more than just a sweet girl." Joseph just smiled. Joseph closed his eyes and remembered Cyndy.

Timothy suddenly spoke and pulled Joseph out of his memory. "So, do you want to continue with your story?" Joseph sat quietly, thinking, 'Lord, what do you want me to do?' After a moment, Joseph continues, "My first real memory, or earliest memory, was when I was four years old. I was at the sitter's house. I don't remember too much, but a dog attacked me. The sitter was sitting on the porch while I played in the yard on my tricycle. She heard some growling, and suddenly a dog was dragging me away. It had me by the top of my head. The sitter ran, and it took some time before she released me from the dog's bite. I have some good scars; that's why I wear my hair a little longer."

Joseph thought, then continued, "I spent a couple of weeks in the hospital. My mom never left my side. After that attack, she quit her job and stayed home to care for me. I don't believe I have gotten over that trauma yet. Whenever I remember it, my heart feels like it will jump out of my chest. I do remember my mom hugging me, which I have never forgotten. When she hugged me, it was so warm and loving. To this day, I can almost smell her perfume. I don't know its name and have never found it anywhere. Then came the day of the accident where I lost my mom." Joseph paused for a couple of moments. He looked at Timothy. He half expected him to be sound asleep, but he wasn't. Timothy had a sympathetic look on his face. Finally, Joseph asked, "Are you sure you want to hear this?"

Timothy nodded his head yes, unable to speak. Joseph continued, "I was seven years old; the car accident was what destroyed my family. We were going on a camping trip. I remember that my mom was singing; she had an angelic voice. She used to sing in the church choir. The car ahead of us was pulling a trailer. The trailer was swaying back and forth, then suddenly, it came loose and forced our car off the road. Dad attempted to avoid the trailer, but he lost control, and the car rolled over. We were on our way up the mountain, and the cliffs were steep."

Joseph paused then continued, "I heard my mom scream, then all I could hear was the ambulance, everything was upside down, and I felt squashed. Dad's voice asked, "Joseph, are you okay? Joseph?" Then I heard him let out a shriek that has haunted my dreams. I heard gurgling. We lost mom that day." It was hard for Joseph not to relive that moment. He cleared his voice and wiped away tears. "I don't remember too much more of that day. I was in shock. The next thing I remember is waking up at the hospital and asking for mom. Dad was in bed next to me. At the funeral, I was pretty much a zombie. I have no other memories of that."

Joseph was silent. Feeling empathetic, Timothy said, "Joseph, I am so sorry for your loss; you must have been a tough kid to survive without any noticeable scars." Joseph looked at Timothy and answered, "My scars were deep inside. I have been doing a lot of healing, but it still hurts immensely." Timothy added, "You look so accomplished and put together. I would never have guessed that you have suffered so much pain. Dude, you are tough."

Joseph smiled, "I can't take all of the credit. Truth be told, I can't take any of the credit. All glory goes to God." Timothy chuckled, "There you go again with God. Where was he in all this pain you suffered?" Joseph smiled, "I used to ask that same question. Now, I know the answer." Timothy asked, "Well, what is it?"

Joseph began, "Do you know that God/YHVH thought of you before you were formed in your mother's womb? He chose you to be here at this time and this moment. YHVH orchestrated you being on this flight, in this seat next to. He created you for His purposes. You have been running for such a long time. YHVH used your mother's death so He could have some of your time." Timothy looked at Joseph with disbelief. "How can you be sure?" Joseph smiled, "I had a flight earlier today, but I heard YAH ask me if I would give up my seat and take a later flight. I did not want to, but He said He would use me for His glory. I thought He had a plan for when I landed but didn't realize it was time to tell my story until you asked." Timothy laughed, "Boy, I am the one that started this. Since I started it, I guess I won't fight it anymore."

Joseph smiled, "Are you ready then?" Timothy smiled, "For what?" Joseph continued, "To forgive yourself." Timothy nodded his head, "Not quite. Tell me more about your story."

Joseph continued, "Life got hard for me. No mom to hold me when things were rough. My dad became an alcoholic, at least in my eyes." Joseph stopped as he realized what he had said. He shook his head, "Wow. I finally spoke those words after all this time. My dad became an alcoholic and was physically abusive. He became a recluse. Dad pushed all my family away, and I did not get to grow up with any of them. At first, my uncles and aunts attempted to come around but finally gave up because my dad would curse at them and throw things. He did not want to be around anyone; that reminded him of his inability to save mom. He was not very nice to me either. He told me on numerous occasions that I only lived with him because mom wanted me. He told me that he never wanted me. Most of the time, I went to school filthy when I was younger, so kids picked on me. I never had lunch money, so I went without quite often. I do not remember too many days of ever feeling full. There were no groceries at home. The refrigerator was full of beer, so I drank to get back at my dad. I soon realized that I was only hurting myself, so I quit drinking. I would steal money from my dad for food. I started breaking into my neighbors' homes and taking food."

Joseph paused, "One night when I was ten years old, one of my neighbors caught me. I thought for sure he would call the police, but he had mercy on me. He sat me down and fed me. He spoke to me about this man named Jesus Christ. I told him that no man loved me. I asked, "Where was he when my mom died?" He told me that my mom loved Jesus. I ran out of his house and never returned. He brought food, but my dad threw it back at him. Dad told him we didn't want or need his charity. He tried a few times and then gave up; you know that man never told on me." Timothy had tears, "Your life sucked, and look at you now. You are dressed in expensive suits and look respectable. How did you do it?"

Joseph laughed, "I can't get ahead of the story. As you can imagine, a kid with no supervision and no food will get into some trouble. I started taking things from stores, but somehow, I was never apprehended. I stole from everyone. One day, I ran away from some kids trying to beat me up when I ran smack into the track coach. Long story short, he recruited me for his track team. He said anyone that can run like that should put it to good use. It was my first year in high school, and I was at a track meet when my coach pulled me aside to tell me that my dad was in the hospital."

Joseph was silent. He gathered himself, "He took me to the hospital, but dad had a massive heart attack, and I didn't get to say goodbye before he passed. My coach reached out to my uncle. The funeral was quiet; not too many people came. Dad had enough money put away to cover the funeral expenses. My uncle sold my dad's house and took me in. When I graduated from high school with a track scholarship, I moved away and only saw my uncle over the summer. It was too hard to return for holidays because I worked full time while in school. Long story short, I graduated college and never went back."

Joseph smiled, "A couple of months ago, while I was on a trip to Denver. I saw a man that looked just like me. I did a double-take. I introduced myself, we chatted for a few minutes, and he said he lived in Denver all his life." Timothy was surprised, "Dude, was that your twin?" Joseph laughed, "No, he is quite a few years older than I am." Timothy laughed, "This is getting kind of freaky, man."

Joseph responded, "You have no idea." Timothy couldn't wait to hear, "Who was he?" Joseph laughed, "Well, we talked for hours, and he spoke a lot about his family. We have been communicating ever since. When I return to the states, I plan on meeting up with him. He is flying out to Los Angeles for a week. I feel he may be related to my birth parents but haven't had the nerve to ask yet." Timothy asked, "Why haven't you asked if anyone gave up a kid?" Joseph smiled, "Trust me, I have wanted to, but how do you ask someone you just met if someone in his family got pregnant and threw away a baby."

Isaiah 55:8

"For My thoughts are not your thoughts,
Nor are your ways My ways," declares the LORD.

Chapter 2 Dinner Time

Lucy appeared from behind the attendant's seating area. She asked, "Please forgive me. I just realized I never brought your water. It's now time for dinner." She handed Joseph water and asked, "Would you prefer breast of Gressingham duck with braised kohlrabi, parsnip mash, caramelized apple, and parsley sauce? Or grilled wild sea bass with warm tartar sauce, potato, Parmesan mousseline, and slow-roasted vine-on cherry tomatoes? They both come with a salad if you'd like?" Lucy smiled at Joseph. Joseph replied, "Thank you for the water. I will take the seabass and salad." Then he glanced at Timothy, who was grinning, ear to ear, "I will take the same, thanks." Lucy turned to help the other passengers. Timothy laughed and whispered, "I see that Lucy may have a special connection with you." Joseph laughed, "It's your imagination. She is smiling at everyone on the flight." Timothy continued, "Yeah, but look at her eyes when she looks at you. It is different from when she looked at me or anyone else. Pay attention, buddy; I think she is sweet on you." Joseph just nodded his head.

Joseph asked, "So what's your story?" Timothy squirmed in his seat, "I don't know. It's not like yours for sure." Joseph quickly answered, "It's not a competition on who has a better or worse life. Your story is yours. Whatever pain or love you have felt is yours and yours only. We all have a story; they are all unique just like us."

Timothy thought, "Well, as I said, I was my mom's favorite kid. She never let me feel like I did not belong. She spent time with each of us, but I always seemed to have more of her time. The other kids were always teasing me about it. They called me mama's boy. I did not care because I knew I loved having all her attention. My dad favored my older brother, and I always felt he did not love me. I know he did love me; that was how I felt as a kid. One day, I had an accident on my bike, and when he found me on the ground, he carried me into the house and lovingly put me in my mother's arms. He ruffled my hair. I remember him telling me that I was brave for not crying. I had my knees and arms all scraped up. My mom fixed me up, bandaged me, and gave me a freshly baked cookie."

Timothy paused for a moment as he remembered his mom's cookies, "Man, she made the best cookies in the entire town. To this day, you cannot buy one as good as hers were. I am the youngest of four kids: my older brother MacKenzie and sisters, Jasmine, and Karen. Karen is a year older than I am. She was my best friend growing up. We were usually together. Karen is the one that ran to get dad when I wiped out on my bike. She called me every day; however, I did not return her calls after dad died. She was like mom, never gave up on me. Karen is the one that called me when mom died. When she called that day, something told me to answer. Karen was courageous and did not cry. I could hear the pain in her voice; however, she spoke very calmly. She said, 'Tim, I need you to come home. Mom is gone. I need you.' I told her I would get the first flight out. So, I booked the first flight out, and here I am. I started drinking the moment she hung up."

Timothy paused, then continued, "I had so much guilt that I hoped that I could numb the pain, but it does not go away. It continues to dig a hole in my soul." Joseph whispered, "Let it go. Say, I forgive myself for not being a better son and brother." Timothy opened his mouth, but nothing came out. Tears filled his eyes as he struggled to speak. Slowly, one tear released, and then others flowed down his face. "I forgive myself. I forgive myself for not being a better son and brother. I forgive myself for running away. I forgive myself for being a coward and not wanting to see the pain that mom and Karen had suffered." Joseph sat quietly, listening.

Timothy began to sob, "I forgive me. Tim, I forgive you. Timothy, I forgive you. Timmie, I forgive you. I forgive myself." Timothy raised his hand to his heart and began to speak to his mom, "I am so sorry, mom. Please forgive me. I am sorry I hurt you more than you deserved. I am so sorry I could not answer your calls. I am so sorry I ran away from you instead of to you. I am so sorry I was not stronger and felt weak. Please forgive me. Please forgive me, mama. Mommy, please forgive me. Mommy, I miss you so much."

Joseph swallowed back the pain he felt himself. He reached over, and placed his hand on Timothy's shoulder, and softly whispered, "Timothy, I am standing in the gap for your mom." Then Joseph continued, "My dearest Timothy. I have always loved you so much. I forgave you the moment you did not answer me. I have never held anything against you, my son. I loved you and never stopped loving you. My love for you grew stronger every day. There is nothing more to forgive. Jesus already paid it on the cross of Calvary. I have loved you from the moment of conception. I love you forever." Joseph knew that the words he spoke were from the Lord. He also knew it was not the time to say anything else. Joseph sat silently, and Timothy sobbed.

Lucy had noticed what was happening, so she handed out everyone else's meals then returned to the men last. She smiled at the men and asked, "Would you like a drink with your meal?" Joseph smiled, "I would like a root beer and water, please." Timothy had pulled himself together and smiled, "I was going to ask for alcohol; however, I will take a coke. Thank you." He turned to Joseph, "I can't believe how much freedom I feel from that. As soon as I spoke the words of forgiving myself, I felt something lift off me. Then the words kind of just gushed out." Joseph smiled, "It doesn't take much for us to feel better, but we carry so much guilt because we either don't know that we must forgive ourselves or we won't. Why did you say you changed your mind about alcohol?" Timothy answered, "I had thought that I needed more alcohol to face my siblings, but suddenly I feel this rush that alcohol doesn't give me. I have not had a coke in many years, but I felt like that is what I wanted. It is weird. My mom never drank, and my dad loved his cokes. Maybe that is the way it is supposed to be, nonalcoholic. I don't know. I feel so good; a sense of peace has come over me."

Lucy returned with the sodas, water, and meals. Once again, Lucy smiled at Joseph, "There is something so familiar about you, but I can't place my finger on it." Joseph smiled, "Maybe you are sensing or discerning my spirit?" Lucy smiled, "Maybe?" Then, as she walked away, she turned and smiled again.

Timothy had noticed, "I told you, she is sweet on you. She lights up even more when she speaks to you." Joseph laughed, "I am not looking for a girlfriend. I need to heal before I even think about that." Timothy asked, "Heal? You have your act together. What more do you need?" Joseph laughed, "Let's enjoy our meal. We have a long flight to talk about healing." Timothy agreed, "Well, my mom always said grace, but I stopped long ago." Joseph smiled, "Do you mind if I do?" Timothy smiled, "Go for it." Joseph quietly prayed, "Papa, thank you for this meal. Thank you for the people you have placed in my life. Bless everyone on this plane and everyone that had a hand in making this meal. Amen." Timothy smiled, "You pray like my mom. She was always so grateful for everything. Thanks, man." Joseph grinned, "Come on, let's enjoy this meal."

Joseph was the first to speak, "Does this food taste better than most airplane food?" Timothy laughed, "That's what I was thinking. I can't say that I have ever enjoyed a meal on a plane, but this is just heavenly." Joseph laughed, "You said it. Heavenly is right. There is so much flavor I can't explain it." Suddenly, the entire plane was murmuring. They all seemed to be enjoying the meal. Laughter broke out, and it was contagious. The flight attendants hurried down the aisles to see what was going on. Joseph suddenly understood. 'Today has been a heavenly experience!'

As he turned to look around, the whole place was glowing. Joseph knew that this was a sign from God. He had never experienced anything like this before. Timothy asked, "What is going on?" Lucy happened to be walking by, "We have no idea. Everyone is laughing and commenting that the food is so delicious. Flavors they have never experienced before. I don't know what's different; it is the same company we always get our food from." The men saw Lucy speak to the pilot. They could overhear her conversation, "Sir, something about the food is making the people laugh uncontrollably. They say that they

15

have never tasted food this good. This joy seems to have overtaken the entire plane. The babies are giggling, and the people are happy." Then, they heard the pilot ask, "Do you think it's food poisoning?" Lucy answered, "If it is, it's a happy poisoning." She laughed. "Keep me abreast of the situation." The captain ordered.

Lucy turned and smiled at Joseph. She came closer and asked, "What is happening?" Joseph smiled, "I am not positive, but I believe everyone is experiencing heaven. I am very new at all of this. But this feels like heaven to me." Lucy smiled, "I knew there was something special about you."

Lucy walked down the aisles to make sure everyone was okay. She enjoyed the laughter and saw that everyone was happy.

Timothy smiled at Joseph, "Well, you will make me change my mind about this God you spoke of, won't you?" Joseph answered, "I can't change your mind. Only you can do that. But He does work in miraculous ways." The men laughed every time one person burst into laughter because the entire plane followed suit. As they finished their meal, Timothy looked at Joseph, "Tell me more about you, please."

Joseph was not sure what he should share next. Joseph stated, "Well, first, why don't you tell me about your dad." Timothy smiled, "He was always kind of distant to me. I saw him with my older brother. They always hugged, and dad used to wrap his arms around him like bear hugs. Mac always wrestled away, and my dad seemed to fight harder to hold on. As Mac got older and taller, my dad was the one that was in the bear hug. I always wanted him to do that to me; however, he was gentler with me. Almost as if I would break if he hugged me." Joseph asked, "Do you know why?" Timothy continued, "It may have been due to my illness as a baby. I was only a few months old when I got pneumonia. I was hospitalized for some time but not sure how long. I was kind of a sickly kid, I guess. I did grow out of it. Maybe that's why my mom favored me."

Joseph asked, "Did you resent your brother's relationship with your dad?" Timothy looked a little puzzled at Joseph, "Jealous? Of my brother? Maybe." Joseph urged him, "What more can you tell me about your dad?" Timothy was feeling uncomfortable, "What do you mean?" Joseph's smile reassured him, "Whatever you want to share." Timothy thought about it, "I know my dad loved me, but I sure didn't feel it. I only wish my dad had done more things with me. Sometimes I just wanted to be treated the same as my brother. He did sports, and I did not. I enjoyed school and my music."

Joseph asked, "Did you excel in school?" He answered, "I did. I loved math and was good at science but not good with blood." Timothy laughed, "I remember Karen and I were playing outdoors, and she got injured. She fell off the swing set, and there was blood everywhere. I passed out. When I came to, Karen was holding my hand. She was laughing at me, but she promised not to tell anyone. However, at dinner, she spilled the beans. Everyone but mom laughed, and I felt like a loser. I know I was only a nine-year-old kid, but it was not a good feeling. I glared at Karen, and she knew I was mad. Mom was the only one that did not ever laugh at me. She seemed to understand that my hospital experience must have traumatized me."

Joseph replied, "She understood you better than anyone else. She also knew that your father's death was tough on you even though you did not feel close to him. You felt you would now never have the chance to feel that father's love and approval." Timothy looked at Joseph, "How did you know that?" Joseph responded, "I heard Papa telling me those things." Timothy looked at him, shocked, "Why do you call Him Papa?"

Joseph smiled, "Well, when I first met Him. I had been crying after mama died; I was seven years old. My father could not hug me for some reason. I knew that my mama believed in God, and she called him Papa. When she taught me to pray, that is how we addressed Him. Anyway, when mama died, I lost my best friend, so I felt all alone. One night I was crying; I usually cried myself to sleep. However, this night I cried out, 'Papa, Papa, why am I all alone? Suddenly, I saw Him. He sat at my bedside and said, 'Yoseph, you are not alone. I am always with you.' I argued, 'I am alone! You took mama away, and daddy does not love me. No one loves me.' He leaned over and hugged me. Papa's hug was so full of love. Nevertheless, that became a distant memory as I got older, and I drifted away. Now, I am back.

Chapter 3 Dreams

Timothy sat in silence, looking straight ahead. Joseph knew that he had to process things. Lucy suddenly stepped beside them and leaned over to Joseph. "Can I say something that is going to sound weird?" Joseph smiled, "Weirder than the entire passengers on the plane laughing uncontrollably?" Lucy laughed, "Okay, maybe it won't sound weird. I remembered why you look so familiar." Timothy snapped out of his thoughts, "Have you met him before?" Lucy smiled and looked at Timothy, "No, not in person. When I was walking back to the front, I remembered a dream I had about a month ago. Joseph, you were in my dream." Joseph laughed, "I was? What was the dream about?"

Lucy suddenly felt embarrassed, "Well, the dream doesn't matter as much as you were in it. That is why you look so familiar to me. Is that weird?" Joseph responded, "No, it is not weird. I have dreamt strangers before I meet them. Sometimes I dream of places, and then suddenly, I get a call to go there. So no, not weird." Lucy smiled, "Thanks. When I remembered the dream, I was afraid that you would think I was weird. I did not want you to think I was hitting on you. That would be very unprofessional." Joseph laughed, "Well, I have a gift for interpreting dreams if you are interested." Lucy smiled, "I couldn't. I am busy but want to share. Maybe after we land." Joseph smiled, "It is a very long flight. We still have another ten hours to go, right?" Lucy answered, "We will see."

Joseph asked, "Timothy, tell me more about your interest in music." Timothy smiled, "Well, after my dad passed away, I stopped writing. I could not think positive thoughts. Everything went dark. Therefore, I focused on my studies instead. I changed my major to business, put my nose to the grindstone, and finished school. I immediately got a job and started traveling worldwide for my company. My excuse for not answering my family was that I didn't have phone service; however, that wasn't always true." Joseph asked, "Are you happy with the career change?" Timothy answered, "Truth be told, no. I enjoy travel and consulting; however, I would rather make music. My music has been so dark even when I have attempted to try music again. I feel the joy has left me."

Joseph waited for the right moment, and then he felt it was time. "Sing something for me." Timothy looked puzzled, "What? Here?" Joseph urged him, "Yes. I can see that a song came to you while we were talking." Timothy smiled, "How did you know that?" Joseph smiled, "Will you believe me if I tell you the first words?" Timothy knew he would never be able to guess the words that came to him. "Yes, tell me." Joseph smiled from ear to ear, "Well, I heard this melody; however, I am not a singer, so therefore I won't sing to you. I heard, 'I will sing you a story, but you won't believe it's true.' Well?" Timothy was amazed, "There's no way you could have heard that. Are you a mind reader?" Joseph laughed, "That is the world's way. I told you, I hear Papa's voice. It may have been an angel's voice this time because it was different but quite beautiful. Maybe Papa allowed me to hear your voice." Timothy was still amazed, "This is hard for me to believe." Joseph replied, "Well, sing, and I will tell you if I heard your voice or not."

Timothy began, "I will sing you a story, but you won't believe it's true. It is a story of my life and how I have been rescued. It started long ago, before I was born — a battle over me. The enemy knew my calling, how I would help those in the darkness. My voice is a breaker. My sound is a sound of freedom. My words are from YHVH, and they will activate you into your calling." Joseph smiled, "That's the voice I heard."

Lucy came and stood beside the men as Timothy sang and hummed along. When Timothy had stopped singing, she whispered, "Timothy, look behind you." When he turned around, he saw that he had an audience. The tears were running down their faces. The plane was silent, and tears continued to flow down their faces. Joseph quietly spoke, "Do you see why the darkness overtook you? It wanted to silence you. You have a voice that needs to be heard." Suddenly someone from the back of the plane shouted, "Sing it again! That was beautiful." Timothy turned and faced the group. "I don't have the words written down. It is something that just happened. Thank you for the encouragement." A little girl stood up and said, "If you sing again, maybe I can see what I saw again." Timothy asked, "What did you see?" The little girl answered, "I could see heaven, and it was so beautiful. So much color and everything moved with sound." Lucy asked, "Did anyone else see anything?" An elderly woman raised her hand, "I didn't see anything; however, I feel so much better. My body was aching before the flight started. When we were all laughing, it went away. However, I feel like the pain will not return since you sang. I don't know how to explain how I know that." Then a man dressed in blue spoke, "I could hear drums as you sang."

Joseph knew that this was another wonder which was happening. Lucy asked, "Anyone else have anything to share?" In the middle of the plane, a young man spoke up, "Earlier, like a couple of minutes before you sang. I swear it is true. I heard what I thought was an orchestra. Harps seemed to be the sound I remember best. The sounds were so beautiful and heavenly." Then a young woman stood up, "I don't know what's happening on this plane. First the food, then the laughter, then you sang and all these people telling you what happened. My experience is weird. I felt like I was on fire. I feel the fire cleansed me and what I felt before the flight is completely gone. I had gotten high before my flight. I had many addictions, and now I do not crave anything. I don't know what's happening, but I am pleased. I was hoping to enter a detox center when I got home, but I don't think I will need it."

Story after story continued for about thirty minutes. Joseph waited until everyone who wanted to share their experiences finished before speaking again. Finally, Joseph asked, "Timothy, do you see how the Lord can use your gift?" Timothy was still having a hard time believing what he had just heard. "I can't get my mind around it. I will have to process it. Let me write down this song before I forget the words.

Chapter 4 Lucy Whispers

Lucy brought Joseph and Timothy water. She whispered, "I can bring whatever snacks or drinks you want. You guys have been quite a blessing for everyone here. I have had people offer to buy whatever snacks you want. Joseph smiled at Lucy. "Do you have a few minutes? I have a word for you." Lucy was surprised, "For me? Sure, I can take a moment." Joseph began, "Lucy, the Lord has created you to illuminate His Light. He has created you to shine brightly in the very dark world. In your eyes, His light shines through without your knowledge. Since you were born, everyone that sees you sees Him. However, He wants you to illuminate His light even brighter and to speak His words. You have a way about you that brings people closer to you. They want what you carry. The joy that radiates from you brings others joy. He wants to take you higher if you will allow Him. He wants to show you heaven so you can share it with others. Not just share it but also bring heaven down. I hear him saying, will you take up your cross and follow me?"

Joseph paused, then continued, "If only you could see yourself the way the Lord sees you. He sees a beautiful creation in golden armor from head to toe. He says I love you. I will always love you and have loved you since the beginning of time." Joseph saw tears running down Lucy's face. He paused, "Lucy, He is waiting for your answer." Lucy had been looking down, then she answered in a whisper, "Yes. I say yes to you, Lord."

Her eyes shifted to Joseph, "In my dream, I was sitting on a bench, waiting for a train. You walked up and sat next to me. I smiled at you but feared that you would see through me. I felt insecure, ugly, and ashamed. I saw how handsome you were and thought you could never love me if you knew how damaged I was. The train pulled up behind us, and we both stood up. You waited for me to walk towards the train, but I turned and walked away. You called out to me. As I turned back to you, you shouted, 'I love you, Lucy!' I froze and could not move. I thought, 'how could a stranger love me. How did you know my name?' You stepped towards me and embraced me. You kissed me and said, 'I love you. I always have.' I began to cry. A strong wind came up, and you wiped my tears away. In that embrace, I felt what love was. In your eyes, I saw what true love was. When I awoke, I was sobbing. I knew that I had never felt that kind of love." Joseph was watching Lucy's face. He gently asked, "Do you need an interpretation?" Lucy nodded her head without speaking. Joseph began in a whisper, "There are a couple of different things I hear; I will give you both. First, you have been waiting for something big to happen in your life. You have never felt worthy. Fearing that I would see all the bad, but Jesus Christ (Yahushuah HaMashiach) has always loved you. There is transparency with Him. He sees and knows all things; nothing can be hidden from Him. Yah has been waiting for you to prepare to get on the ride or train; He wants to take you on. The ministry He has for you will be very powerful and unstoppable. Holy Spirit will be right there with you. The second thing I hear. He shows you people in your dreams like myself, which He will introduce to you. These people will see what you carry. You will show or teach them the love of Yahushuah HaMashiach. Your ministry is about Love, His Love. Allow Him to teach you; His love is so powerful. It will move mountains. His Love brings His compassion into all things and heals all wounds. No one is too damaged for Him."

Lucy began to laugh. She said, "You would not believe how embarrassed I felt when you first offered to Interpret my dream. When I remembered the dream and you kissing me, I was afraid you would think I was weird or forward. I was afraid you would judge me." Timothy interrupted, "May I say something?" Lucy looked at him, "Sure." Timothy began, "First, let me say. I have never done this before. I do not interpret dreams, but I have a strong feeling or sense that there is more to this dream." Joseph smiled, "Timothy, that is how it all begins. You get a sense or impression, and you must decide if you are hearing God, yourself, or something else. Go ahead, no judgment."

Timothy began again, "Lucy, I feel that Joseph in your dream represents Joseph as your future husband, not just Jesus. You have been waiting for the man of your dreams. He saw the good and beauty in your spirit through your eyes. I admit I teased him; however, I could see that there was more. He had no lust when he saw you. I saw that it was pure love." Timothy glanced over at Joseph, then at Lucy. Lucy laughed, "I heard you tease him. However, you are correct; I saw purity in the way that he looked at me. He always looked into my eyes. I saw a gentleness or softness in his spirit." Joseph interrupted, "Now you guys are going to make me blush. I did see the Lord in your eyes." Timothy continued, "Joseph, I do not know if you understand the chemistry, I feel between the two of you, but I feel this electricity going through me just being between you two." Joseph looked at Lucy and Timothy, "Timothy, you are feeling Holy Spirit. But, Lucy, I must ask, Do you know the Lord personally?" Lucy laughed, "Only since my dream a month ago."

Timothy laughed, "Okay. I want what you both have. I feel awesome; this is a different kind of high. I can't get over this electricity." People behind and beside them listened and were now entering the conversation. The woman sitting closest to Timothy laughed, "I feel like I am on fire! What is this?" Joseph answered, "That is Holy Spirit you are experiencing." She asked, "Why haven't I felt this before? I have been a Christian all my life." Joseph was unsure how to answer, "I am not sure because I am a newborn in the Messiah Yahushuah or Christ Jesus. I can only say that this is all new to me." Finally, she asked, "Why do you say Yahushuah and not Jesus?" Joseph smiled, "Well, I studied the Hebrew language, and I wondered why anyone would translate a name. As I sought the Lord or YHVH, I read that the Torah went through four major translations. First from Hebrew to Greek, then Greek to Latin, then Latin to English. If you travel to other countries, would you be called by any other name? My name is Joseph, whether I go to Mexico, Africa, or China. So, I felt I should call the Lord by His name in Hebrew." She stated, "That makes a lot of sense, but if we never have learned or studied other languages like Hebrew, how are we to know?" Joseph answered, "Great point. Now that you know, does it make you want to learn more about our Lord and His name?" She smiled, "I guess so."

Timothy interrupted, "Sorry to interrupt this conversation, but I still feel this electricity." Lucy laughed, "Do you want it to end?" Timothy quickly responded, "No! I want to know what to do. Am I supposed to do something?" Joseph answered, "Do you hear or see that you are to do something?" "I guess I am," Timothy stated. "I have a feeling I am supposed to touch someone. That sounds weird, right?" Lucy answered, "I had a dream once that I was on fire and heard the Lord tell me to touch someone. So, who are you supposed to touch?"

Timothy looked around, "I think it is that person three rows back." Joseph coached him, "Okay. Ask him if he is having pain. If he says yes, ask if it's okay for you to pray and lay your hands on him." Timothy headed toward the man. As he approached him, he asked, "Sir, this may sound weird but are you having pain?" The man asked, "How did you know?" Timothy answered, "By the way, my name is Timothy, but you can call me Tim. I am not sure, but when I saw you, I felt a pain in my heart." The man responded, "Hi, Tim. My name is Nick. I started having pain in my chest about 10 minutes ago. I thought it was all the laughter, but that is not possible. That was so pleasant." Timothy continued, "May I place my hands on your chest? You can put your hands under my hands, so it doesn't feel weird." Nick looked at him, puzzled, "What are you doing?" Timothy answered, "I feel like the pain will go away when I place my hand on your chest." Nick replied, "I have nothing to lose."

Nick placed his hand on his chest as if he was getting ready to say the pledge of allegiance. Timothy looked at Joseph, "Now what? Just ask the Father to heal him. Timothy began pausing between words, "God. Papa. I do not know what to say. You can heal him. You can take the pain away." Then Timothy suddenly started speaking as if he had been doing this all his life, "In the name of the Messiah, Jesus Christ. I command pain to leave. I command healing of Nick's heart and entire body." Nick suddenly jerked, "Whoa!" Timothy did not skip a beat, "Go from him now in Jesus' name." Nick looked at Timothy, "Wow! I felt the fire going through your hands into my hands and body. The feeling is amazing! Wow! God is real! I feel like a new man! I believe! I had doubts before, but now I believe."

Lucy asked, "Is there anyone else that is having pain?" No one answered. Lucy then gave a word of knowledge, "Someone here, in this row, has eyesight issues. Don't be afraid; God wants to do a miracle today and heal you." A woman raised her hand, "My baby cannot see." Lucy looked at the baby with compassion and began to cry. "I hear the Lord saying that you have felt so much guilt and pain because of your baby's condition. You have asked the Lord if you did something wrong while pregnant. He says no. I had a plan a long time ago to heal on this flight." Lucy looked at Timothy, "Place your hand on the baby's eyes." Timothy obeyed. The mother was crying. When Timothy removed his hands, the baby looked at him and smiled. The mother picked up her baby, and the child reached out to her face and laughed. The mother cried, "She has never looked at me like this before. She can see! Thank you." Timothy smiled, "I didn't do anything. God is healing. It is all God." Joseph added, "To God be the glory. When you tell people what happened, give God all the glory. We are obedient and willing to be used by God."

Joseph looked at Timothy and Lucy, "You hear the Lord's voice. Always be willing to do His work. Always tell those who come across your path that all the Glory belongs to God. The kingdom of God is at hand." Joseph continued, "Timothy, you have always known the Lord. It is time to rededicate your life to Him."

Timothy laughed, and he looked around, "Does anyone else want to give your lives to the All-Mighty God? If you do, repeat after Joseph. Joseph? Would you lead me through the prayer?" Joseph smiled, "I would be honored."

Joseph looked around him as he saw some people close their eyes. He began pausing after every section, "Our Father who art in heaven. Hallowed be thy name. Thy kingdom come thy will be done. On earth, as it is in heaven. I have sinned. Please forgive me. Forgive my words that have hurt others. Yahushuah, Jesus, I rededicate my life to you. Be my Lord and Savior. I choose to follow you. Help me to be the person you created me to be. I ask this in the name of the Messiah Yahushua HaMashiach. Amen.

Joseph looked around, and he saw almost the entire flight with tears in their eyes. He headed back to his seat when he felt a hand reach out and touch him. He turned to see who it was and saw an older man. He asked, "Sir, may I help you with something?" The man spoke in a shaky voice, "I saw you walk onto the plane. I knew that you carried something special, and then the laughter started. You were in such deep thought; that you were almost hiding. I saw the pain you carried; however, the glory that surrounded you was even greater. I pray today's experience that you have witnessed is enough to keep you focused on the Word and increase your faith. Give Him everything as He eases that pain. He will sweep away all the junk and fill you with His glory." Joseph began to thank him, but he disappeared. Joseph looked up at Timothy and Lucy, but they had their backs to him. He looked at the people around him; however, they turned their heads and were in conversation with their friends or neighbors.

Joseph turned to walk away when he heard that voice again. He stopped and listened, "Yes. The answer is yes." Joseph smiled; he had not even finished the thought. He had thought, 'Did I just meet an angel?' His thoughts continued, 'I wonder how many times I had spoken to angels?'

Chapter 5 Plane on Fire

Joseph was suddenly feeling tired. He sat down and closed his eyes. Joseph saw the plane on fire. He opened his eyes and looked out the window. Joseph asked, 'Yahushuah HaMashiach is that spiritual fire? Or are we going to be in trouble?' He heard, 'Rest. Fear not.' Joseph heard these words for the first time; however, deep sleep overtook him. He began to dream.

Joseph saw an angel smile at him. Joseph asked, "Who do you serve?" The angel responded, "YHVH, EL ELYON." He extended his hand and took hold of the angel. He was flying. Joseph was in outer space. He could see the earth below him. Then he began to get closer to earth. Joseph was flying over the tops of trees. Suddenly, he saw a house. It looked like a party. There was youth everywhere. Then Joseph saw her. She was about 14 or 15 years old, had on jeans and a blouse with a varsity athlete's jacket. The jacket was blue with white sleeves. The young girl had her hair up in a ponytail. He looked over at the angel, and he was communicating but not with words. It was telepathic communication. He heard him say, 'Just watch and see.' Everyone in the house was drinking, including this young girl. Joseph heard the girl tell her friend, 'Don't leave me alone. We need to stay together. Okay?' Her friend responded, 'Sure.' Joseph could tell that she would not honor her end of the agreement. People kept pushing glasses of alcohol at the girl. Then Joseph saw her stumble into the young man's arms. He walked her over to a room. She passed out. Then he saw the young man start to undress her. Joseph looked at the angel and said, 'we have to help her.' The angel shook his head.

Next, the room went dark. Joseph saw a cell; he was flying through space. Joseph saw a bright light, almost like a lightning bolt. It was the most brilliant light he had ever seen. There was a thunderous sound or explosion. He ran into something substantial, and suddenly he saw the multiplication of cells. Joseph heard a loud roaring voice say, 'attah, yachiyd Yoseph.' Joseph understood the voice to say, 'Thou art my beloved son Joseph." As the cells multiplied, he could hear the young girl's voice, 'I do not know what happened. How could I be pregnant? I do not want this baby."

These words continued to echo as the cells multiplied. Suddenly, Joseph knew that he was the baby. Then Joseph started to feel pressure. Something strange was happening to him; he felt intense pressure and pain. The force made him kick, punch, and he tried to scream, but no sounds came out. There was so much pressure that his head felt like it would explode. 'Whoa! The light was very bright! Suddenly the warmth was gone, and it became frigid.' Joseph thought to himself, 'Where am I.' Suddenly, he saw a beautiful face; oh, it was the face of the young girl. She was crying. She wrapped Joseph in her athletic jacket and hurried around the corner. She placed him with such gentleness in a huge metal box. Joseph suddenly understood, 'This is the infamous garbage bin.' Joseph heard her cry and saw her tears land on his cheek.

Joseph opened his eyes. Timothy was sitting next to him. Timothy spoke first, "Are you okay?" Joseph looked at him, not knowing what to say. Finally, Timothy asked, "Dude, you look like you will be sick. You, okay?" Joseph gathered himself, "Yeah, how long was I sleeping?" Timothy responded, "Only about fifteen or twenty minutes. Why?" "I just had the coolest dream. What else happened?" Timothy asked, "Do you mean with the healing fest?" Joseph smiled, "Yeah. What did I miss?" Timothy laughed, "Well, we had a couple of people that were deaf, and now they hear. Do you remember the blind baby?" Joseph nodded. Timothy continued, "She started talking too. This older man got up and walked around without pain. A man in the back said his back pain was completely gone. It was very cool! Why did you get tired?"

Joseph smiled, "Papa wanted to show me something." Timothy was eager to hear, "Well, what was it?" Joseph quickly glanced around the plane, "The first time, I closed my eyes, I saw the plane on fire. I asked Papa if that was spiritual or literally? He told me to rest and fear not." Timothy laughed, "Well, the fire is spiritual and literal because it felt so hot here. His Fire was moving through the plane." Joseph laughed. "It was pretty hot in here. I do not believe that it was the heat that made me tired. I think it was Papa. He had something significant to show me." Timothy added, "Well, what did he show you?"

Joseph grabbed his cell phone and began to record. Joseph lowered his voice and whispered as if what he was about to share was top secret. "An angel took me. He held my hand as we flew. At first, I saw the earth. I must have been in outer space. He took me so far out that the earth looked so small. There was a bright ring around the earth. It seemed to glow. The blue was a color I cannot even explain to you. The vision or dream was so vivid and vibrant. Then we started flying towards the earth. The next thing I saw, we had entered the atmosphere. Suddenly I was flying through the clouds. Then I am flying over the trees. Finally, we arrived at a house. I noticed that the house owners must be wealthy because of the manicured lawn and the pruned trees. It looked impeccable." Joseph looked at Timothy, who is sitting with his mouth open. Joseph laughed and reached over and closed his mouth. He asked teasingly, "Shall I continue?" Timothy laughed, "I am in awe of this God we serve. Yes, please continue."

Joseph took a deep breath, "I saw my biological mother. She was about fourteen or fifteen. My mother was so young and beautiful. She had attended a party; I am sure she was not supposed to be there. She wore blue jeans, a white and pink blouse, and a blue and white athletic jacket. I could see that she looked very nervous. She was with her friend who promised not to leave her alone. However, the girls did end up separating. The people at the party kept handing her glasses of drinks. My mother would take a drink occasionally, but someone must have put something in her drink because she was very drunk or drugged. I also saw the man that assaulted her. He is my biological father."

Joseph had to pause a moment. "Then I was in the darkness and moving very quickly. The sounds were like a rushing river and deafening. I saw that I was a cell. Then there was a bright light, and I crashed into a bigger cell. It was like a lightning bolt. At first, the sound was so loud that I could not hear then came this quiet and calm. I think that was the moment. I heard a voice that sounded like thunder. I believe it was in Hebrew, but I understood it in English. I heard, 'attah, yachiyd Yoceph' but understood 'Thou art My beloved son Joseph.' There was a splash of color, and multiplication began. I saw the division of cells and multiplication repeatedly. It felt like I was in this cycle for a long time."

Joseph paused, then continued, "The sounds were incredible. I do not know how to explain them. First, it was whoa, shsh, oogaoo, cuoo, quoaish. The next thing I saw is that I was beginning to form into a baby: the sounds of muscle, nerves, tendons, bones, all growing, were indescribable. Then, I heard my mother saying that she does not want me. She did not know how it happened. But she kept saying that she did not want me. I could hear and feel her pain. She cried a lot. I do not know whom she was talking to, but she kept saying that she did not want me. I am not sure how many times I heard that." Joseph paused as he processed what he saw, heard, and experienced. Finally, Timothy asked, "Are you okay, dude?" Joseph nodded and said, "I can't believe what I experienced. It is humbling."

Joseph continued after a few minutes. "Then, I started to feel pressure. Something strange was happening. Not that what I saw and felt was not strange; however, this was a different strange. The sounds were terrifying. The sounds were similar to those in a scary movie — haunting sounds. I felt pressure and pain that was almost unbearable. The pressure made me kick and punch. I felt like I was fighting for my life. My heart was racing almost felt like it was jumping out of my body. I kept kicking and punching for a long time. I screamed, but no sounds came out. My scream was deafening in my head; however, I knew the sound did not leave my mouth. There was so much pressure that my head felt like it would explode. Then, Whoa! The light was very bright! I could not keep my eyes open. Suddenly, it was super cold. I felt like my body was shaking uncontrollably. Then I saw her again. She was beautiful, and it was the face of the young girl. She was crying. She kept telling me she was sorry. Finally, she wrapped me in her athletic jacket and hurried around the corner. She kissed my cheek and then placed me in a huge metal box with such gentleness. I understood at that moment; it was the garbage bin. I could hear her crying as she walked away from me. The sound of her crying eventually faded and ended. I was alone in darkness again, but this time it was quiet. That's when I woke up."

Timothy was the first to speak, "That is awesome! I do not know anyone who has ever experienced their life like that. How do you feel?" Joseph sat quietly, then responded, "I guess I am shocked. I always wondered who my mother was and why she gave me up. I can no longer wonder. I know the truth. I am a result of rape and drugs." Joseph was having a hard time processing. Timothy quickly jumped in, "Wait a minute. You can't look at the bad stuff, isn't that what you told me? Look at the good. If you had not been born, none of these people would have received today's blessing. You would not have been here for me today. What if I had told you this story? What would you have said to me?"

Joseph smiled at Timothy, "Okay, grasshopper. You are right; I have a purpose. Besides, I heard Papa's voice at conception. The Word says that He knew me from my mother's womb." Joseph smiled at Timothy, "So, how are you feeling?" Timothy responded, "Better yet now how are YOU feeling?" Joseph laughed, "Oh, so you will make sure I am, okay? Well, to be perfectly honest. I must process the dream. I know that this experience is one that I will not forget. I also know how my biological parents look. So someday, if I happen to run into them, I will know who they are. Of course, they will be much older."

Timothy laughed. "How does it feel to know that your mother cried because of giving you up?" Joseph thought for a moment, "I feel relieved in a strange way. I know she was very young and probably hid the pregnancy. I am not sure how one could hide it because she was skinny. Not anorexic but thin. When I was in the womb and heard her say she did not want me, I could feel so much pain. It was as if my heart broke; I felt unwanted in the womb. That was a difficult feeling as a baby. I felt a stabbing pain with a sharp object in my heart. I feel okay now, but when I was dreaming, that pain was real."

Timothy waited a moment, "Tell me what you mean about the sounds you heard." Joseph asked, "Which ones?" Timothy answered, "All of them!" Joseph thought for a moment, "Well, outer space was interesting. The sound was nothing yet incredibly loud. It was as if I could hear the stars, planets, and all the light. The color was incredible. It was as if it was making sounds. As I said earlier, the sounds are difficult to explain. However, it was something like, whoa whoa, swshsh, quoaoo, cumaloo, woooo, I know that is not even close to it, but that is the best I can do."

Joseph paused, then continued, "As we traveled towards the earth, the speed made my ears feel plugged from all the noise. When we entered the atmosphere, I could hear a sonic boom. I was not hot or cold. When we went through the clouds, it was so calming. As we traveled over the trees and houses, I heard all the dogs and people talking. It was weird to hear so many conversations at once. The music in the house was too loud to hear what all the conversations were, but I could hear her. It was as if I focused on her. I never heard anyone speak her name." Joseph stopped speaking as he thought about her. 'If only I knew her name.' He thought to himself. Joseph was trying to burn her image in his mind. He was hoping to keep that innocent face fresh in his mind. After all, this was his mother. He thought to himself, 'I will try to sketch their faces but mostly her face.'

After a few minutes of silence, Timothy inquired, "A penny for your thoughts. Were your thoughts on the rape?" Joseph snapped out of his thoughts, "Gosh no. I did not see it, so I do not want to think about that. Let me see, the sounds of the cells multiplying were incredible. Have you ever made a meatloaf?" Timothy looked puzzled, "No." Joseph continued, "Well, you have to mix the ingredients with the meat, and usually, I do it by hand. The ground beef makes a 'ta' sound as you mix the ingredients between your fingers. The sound you hear is the closest sound I can think of that sounds like the cells multiplying. It was loud and strange. In the womb, outside sounds were muffled and weird. However, the sound of my mother's voice was loud and clear. I felt like I vibrated in the womb when she laughed, cried, or spoke. She had a gentle way of speaking; however, the words were sometimes deadly. I was happy when she was happy. I was sad when she was sad. When she cried, I felt that I would die. Sometimes, she would place her hands on her stomach, and I felt her warmth. When she sang, I felt like I was flying."

Joseph looked at Timothy, "If mothers only knew what their babies go through. I don't think anyone would purposely be sad or speak offensive words." Timothy quietly spoke, "Maybe, it would also be important for us to know what mothers go through so that we don't hurt our mothers who will do anything for their kids. Why don't we all experience what you just experienced?" Joseph responded, "Do you think it would make a difference?" Timothy answered, "Probably not. When we are suffering, we do not think about anyone else. We are too busy wallowing in our pain. We are too busy licking our wounds to see what others may or may not be feeling."

Joseph saw where the conversation was going, so he changed the subject. "When I started to feel the pressure. I heard creepy sounds. I believe I heard the demonic. I think they were trying to kill me. I could not make out what they said, but it was creepy. I have not had time to process it; also, I strongly believe that something was trying to kill me. My little head felt like it would explode with intense pain. All I can say is that it was creepy. I do not remember being fearful. At the moment I was born; that is when the pain subsided. The light was so bright, and that is when the cold hit me. I do not know how long I was out of the womb when she wrapped me in her jacket, and when I saw her face. It was as if time had stopped. I looked at her; she was crying. This time her crying did not hurt as much. Not sure why other than maybe it was because I lost that umbilical cord connection. I remember feeling some sadness about her crying because it sounded familiar, but the pain was not there." Timothy asked, "Did you feel scared?" Joseph answered, "No, there was a calm about me. I did not cry out. I may have understood what was happening. A part of me feels that I somehow knew that Papa would look after me. I felt peace when I awoke. Shocked but peace."

Timothy responded, "That is an intense dream. That's weird that it only took fifteen to twenty minutes to dream all of that." Joseph answered, "I don't know that this dream took that long. We get so much information in dreams that it would be impossible to retain everything. I may have forgotten something; however, I am hopeful that I will remember later. I am always amazed at how vivid the dreams are most times. There are times that I do not remember a thing, but I know I was dreaming. Papa wanted to show me this so I can get over being abandoned." Timothy looked puzzled, "What? You felt abandoned?"

Joseph smiled, "Yes, of course. Left at birth, then my mom died. Dad never treated me as if he cared. Then he died. My uncle attempted to step in, but it was too late. I had already felt too much pain. I never felt that I could trust him. It was not his fault; I was trying to protect myself. I had too much pain and was never able to deal with it. I didn't have the kind of help one needs. I needed a real Father, and that is where Papa came into my life. Then Ruach Haqodesh stepped in to teach and comfort me. Yahushuah HaMashiach is the best friend I longed for." Timothy thought for a moment, "I see. That is what I also needed all this time. I ran away for such a long time and just dug a deeper hole if only I had known all this when I was a kid. Then, I may not have missed out on my mom and siblings."

Chapter 6 Finish Your Story

Joseph sat reflecting on everything that had taken place on this flight. Finally, he asked, 'Papa, what now?' He heard, 'You haven't finished your story.' Joseph glanced over at Timothy and smiled. Timothy had his eyes closed and appeared to have fallen asleep.

Lucy reappeared and walked over to him. "Do you need anything? Are you cold? I can bring a blanket." Joseph answered, "Thanks. I am doing fine. How are your passengers doing?" Lucy was surprised at the question, "They all seem to be peacefully resting. Even the babies are quiet. This experience has been the most amazing flight I have ever worked on. I am so happy that you are here." Joseph smiled, "You know it wasn't my idea. Originally, I was scheduled for an earlier flight when they needed someone to give up a seat. Then, I heard I was supposed to be the one. Papa said it was for His glory. He sure has shown up today. He does most days, but today was special." Lucy grinned, "He does enjoy seeing you in action. Would you please excuse me? Someone needs my assistance. Please turn on your light if you need anything."

As she walked away, Joseph thought about his high school sweetheart, Cyndy. Until now, she had been the only one who knew how rough his life had been. He smiled as he remembered his nickname for her - Cinderella. Her favorite color was yellow, and she always smelled so sweet. He chuckled to himself.

He felt Timothy stir. He looked over at him, and he was sitting up. Timothy looked over at his new friend, "Did you get in a few Z's?" Joseph replied, "No, I have been thinking." Timothy pressed, "About what? Are you still processing your dream?" Joseph responded, "No, just life."

"What about life?" Timothy asked. Joseph laughed, "Haven't you gotten tired of speaking to me? We have been on this flight for five hours." Timothy smiled, "Really? Nope. You are the first person I have enjoyed speaking to." Joseph shook his head and smirked. "Will you answer if I ask you a tough question?" Timothy smiled, "Of course, I will. I have nothing to hide. I am an open book as of today." Joseph had a somber look on his face. "Tell me what it felt like to have your mom hug you."

Timothy was shocked at the question. "Dude? Are you serious?" Joseph shook his head. Timothy continued, "Well, her hug was so warm as a kid. Her voice was soothing and calmed me in my time of trouble. There were times when I was sick, and her hug made me feel better. She was gentle in all her ways when it came to me. I remember she would fix my shirt and tuck it into my pants. She would gently fix the collar. She would run her hand through my hair and softly say something like, 'Love you, baby boy.' She always gently touched my cheek. I never understood how her hands could feel so warm, but now I do. She never stopped stroking my hair. I often thought about that when I was not responding to her. I wondered if she missed that as much as I did. I must share something else."

Timothy looked at Joseph, "Remember I said I had a gut feeling that I needed to answer my sister's call?" Joseph nodded. "I had a dream that morning. I dreamt that my mom and I were talking at her house. She told me about her mother, who passed when I was a baby. She was telling me how much she missed her. She said that she was lucky to know her so well. They were terrific friends. Best of friends when she was older." Timothy stopped talking.

Joseph waited and said, "Look, I am sorry for your loss. I was trying to remember what it felt like to have mom hold me, but it had been so long. Every memory seems to have disappeared or most likely faded out of existence. As you spoke, I could almost feel mom's hugs. Thanks for sharing. I see how hard this was for you."

Joseph changed the subject a little. "What was it like to grow up with a brother and sisters?" Timothy smiled and laughed, "It was a huge pain! I can only imagine that it must have been very lonely for you. Our house was full of laughter and fighting. Someone was always arguing about toys or clothes. But even though there was fighting, I think there was more laughter than fighting. I always had a friend in my sister, so I could still hang out with her even when the older ones picked on me."

Joseph smiled, "I had always hoped that my dad would remarry so I would have siblings, but that didn't happen. In school, I did not have many friends. I was never sad, even though kids still seemed to bully or try to beat me up. The teachers were not too much better. They always sent notes home for my dad, and I got into trouble. I never had any help with my studies, so at first, I struggled. I finally did better. The lunchroom people were tough too. Whenever my dad forgot to pay for my lunch ticket, they would point it out and make a huge fuss. I finally just started skipping lunch. I would excuse myself to go to the restroom and never make it to the lunchroom. It did not seem to matter what I would do. I could not seem to have very many friends. I attempted to be a class clown, but kids thought I was a goof-off. I kept quiet then kids thought I was aloof. I could not be too nice because people walked all over me. Being a nerd did not work either because the jocks attempted to put me in my place. However, they were not successful since I was athletic. I was a fighter but never became a bully. Maybe the fighter in me was in my DNA from the start. I had to fight for my life as a baby. I guess I was born a fighter."

Timothy laughed, "You were created to fight. This fight is unlike fistfights; it is a spiritual battle. From what I have seen, I have to say that you are doing a great job." Joseph laughed, "I guess I have been equipped since the beginning of time. I just needed to understand what I was created to do. Everything is in His timing. He won't waste what we learn along the way."

Joseph asked, "What was your high school experience like?" Timothy thought, then answered, "Well, it was easy because I had my sister. Karen showed me the ropes. She was never ashamed of having her little brother around. That was cool. I was a little brother to most of her friends. I also believe that her boyfriends' saw me as their little brother. Karen commanded respect for us both. She quickly straightened them out if anyone attempted to get on my case. Karen was a leader; very outgoing, cheery, and full of life. She loved science. I thought she would be a doctor, but she decided that she loved kids more, so she became a teacher. Karen is a science teacher in our hometown. She stayed close to mom. Anyway, my senior year was fun. I ended up becoming a leader by her example. I was not as outgoing as she was. When I went off to college, she was the one that called me daily. Mom took it hard when I did not come home after dad passed away; I could not stand to see her that way. I saw and felt her sadness, so I ran away and never returned until now."

Joseph smiled, "What matters is that you are coming home now. Your sister will need your help with things. Is she married?" Timothy looked at Joseph, "She was married. She has a little one but has been on her own for a while." Joseph added, "Then she needs you more than before. Is this the first time you're meeting the little one?" Timothy smiled, "Yes. She is a beautiful little girl. Karen always texts me pictures." Joseph added, "What's her name?" Timothy laughed, "Can you believe she named her Timmie Rae?" Joseph answered, "Sounds like she must love you to have given her your name." Timothy smiled, "I guess so. Timmie will be teased because of her masculine name." Joseph smiled, "I don't know. I like it. She will have to be tough to deal with what the world is like today. She will be a fighter."

Timothy laughed, "Maybe you can come with me. Can you take a couple of days off?" Joseph shook his head, "Not sure this is the right time. You need to face this thing on your own, although it would be an honor to come to meet your family. Maybe we can make plans for that." Timothy continued, "I feel like I have known you all my life. Is that weird?" Joseph smiled, "We are supposed to be like family, so that's not weird." Timothy quietly spoke, "You know more about me than anyone else except my sister." Joseph laughed, "Well, you know more about me than anyone else. We must be willing to be open to be used by YAH."

Joseph shared a little more, "High school was hard for me. My track coach recruited me at the beginning of my ninth-grade year. I was running away because I did not want to receive a suspension from school for fighting. My dad had threatened to do physical harm if I got into another fight, so I ran. Coach Thompson was coming out of his classroom. He taught Honors Algebra and Physics. Coach Thompson was the closest man that came to being a father to me. He knew that things were bad at home and never asked. He always had food for me. I usually found money in my backpack but never asked who put it there."

Joseph remembered, "I was just grateful that I could buy food instead of stealing it. After my dad passed away, I moved in with my uncle, which offered food and healthier home life. However, I was not home much. I would stay out late and get up early. I ran every day in the morning and evening. I ended up getting a part-time job to have extra cash in my last year of school. I was looking at going out of state for college so the coach would pay for my applications when I did not have enough money. He called me every week when I left for college. The few times I returned home; he was the first person I went to see. He would always have me over for dinner with his family. His kids were never very friendly to me; however, his wife was very nice. I worked in college and was always blessed with quick promotions and received pay increases often. As I look back, I see the favor on my life even though life was hard."

Timothy was not surprised to hear his story. "You never noticed how favored you were?" Joseph responded, "No, I guess I was too busy trying to prove myself. I did not want to be that guy that had a chip on his shoulder. I just thought it was all me." Timothy smiled, "Yeah, when I sat down today. I felt at peace. I cannot even explain how I knew you were safe to spill my story. I feel like you carry peace and calm." Joseph looked at him, "What do you mean?" Timothy answered, "Your presence, or maybe the better word, is your the spirit. You just ooze peace and calm." Joseph replied, "I didn't realize that. I was a super angry kid, but I felt that anger left me when I went off to college. Then, a couple of months ago, I experienced peace as I had never felt before. The day that Papa came to me was when my life did a complete 360."

Chapter 7 Match Maker

Timothy asked, "So are you seeing someone?" Joseph laughed, "What do you mean? I can see you." Timothy pressed, "We have been sitting here talking all this time. Consequently, we haven't spoken about our personal lives." Joseph shook his head and answered, "Well, this has been very personal for me. To answer your question, no, I don't have a girlfriend." Timothy asked, "Are you looking?" Joseph responded with a laugh, "Not really. Who are you trying to set me up with?" Timothy continued, "I don't even know how old you are. I am guessing my age, 30." Joseph smiled, "Well, I am a little younger than you. I am 26. What were you thinking?" Timothy answered with a laugh, "That's not too young for my sister."

Joseph laughed, "I don't think your sister would appreciate you trying to set her up." Timothy quickly responded, "I am just looking out for you. How about Lucy?" Joseph chuckled, "Well, again, I am not looking right now. I am quite busy. My priority right now is to see what I need to do next. I want to leave my life open for now." Timothy chuckled, "Are you sure? Lucy is cute." Joseph shook his head, "She seems adorable, but I think I can handle my love life. Thanks for your concern. How about you? Do you have someone special in your life?"

Timothy laughed, "I don't, but I am looking. I have always wanted to have a family. I have been so busy making a name for myself that I have ignored that part of my life. Do you have someone in mind for me?" Timothy could not stop laughing. Joseph looked around, "So what do you look for in a girl?" Timothy suddenly got serious, "I think I will have to get back to you on that. I have a feeling that my criteria will change after today." Joseph smiled, "Yes, I believe things will be different."

"Do you wonder why you had such a difficult life compared to other people?" Timothy was serious again. Joseph was thinking about his answer. "You wouldn't believe how much I have thought about this. The answer I keep hearing Papa say is that the enemy knew my calling, and so he attempted to take me out. So, about a month ago, I asked Papa to show me where he was at each attack." Timothy was very intrigued, "Well, did He show you?" "Yes, He did," Joseph responded.

"The first thing He showed me was when I was born. He was standing beside my biological mother. He told her to go to the hospital, but she was so afraid of someone finding out her secret. Then I saw the sanitation worker. He was whispering in His ear to look inside the garbage can. Next, he showed me the hospital. There he held the hands of the surgeons and nurses as they cared for me. He also walked with my mom in the NICU and led her right to me." Joseph paused in thought. Timothy recalled the dream Joseph had had an hour ago. "You said that you heard a thunderous voice tell you your name. He has had a plan for you all along."

Joseph shook his head and continued, "That was a cool dream. It was great to see myself as a baby so tiny and innocent. To see my mother hold and sing to me was reassuring. She sat with me every day, and I know she was praying for me as she rocked me back and forth. The nurses could not get her to go home. They ended up calling my dad to come to take her home. Do you know how some people say that animals imprint? Well, that is how it seemed to be for my mom. I imprinted on her heart. I saw her crying when she left me. Next, He showed me the dog attack. Papa had whispered in my ear, instructing me to go inside when I did not listen. He whispered in the sitter's ear that it was time for me to go inside the house. Neither listened to his voice. Papa gave her supernatural strength to fight the dog when the dog attacked me. He then placed his hands in the surgeons' hands when they operated on me." Timothy was amazed at what he was hearing, "Wow! I had no idea how hard He works to keep us safe."

Joseph nodded his head in agreement and continued, "Next was the car accident. YHVH whispered in my ear that I had to go pee. When I told my dad, he told me to wait for a few more minutes. YHVH then whispered in my mom's ear to tell him to pull over. Dad did not listen. As the car swerved and rolled over, YHVH had his hand on me. I saw Him sitting next to me; however, I went into shock and passed out. I asked why He did not save my mom. He said that her assignment on earth was complete. She was to rescue me and love me. I asked him why not take dad instead. He told me that dad was supposed to learn to be a good father but instead, he chose to retreat into his sorrow. Papa showed me all the people He sent to help my dad. Unfortunately, he refused the help. He told me we all have choices; dad refused to forgive himself. Dad blamed himself for his wife's death. He knew he should have pulled over for me to pee. Papa never forces us. He gently encourages us." Timothy asked, "Why not just force us to do the right things?" Joseph smiled, "YHVH gave us free will. He wants us to do what is right. He will never force us. We would be puppets in His hands. Papa wants a relationship with us."

Joseph continued, "When I decided to drink the beer in my refrigerator. I had a choice not to yet; I still did it. I soon realized that it did not hurt dad because he did not notice me. I did not want to hurt myself. Every time I stole something, Papa was there telling me not to. When I was getting into fights, He was there telling me to walk away. I finally obeyed and ran. He showed me how the coach was getting ready to leave, and He delayed him for me."

"I didn't tell you that I grew up in the Mid-West in rural communities. When I was in high school, I drove home in a snowstorm and went into the ditch. I was waiting for someone to come by and pull me out, but no one was coming. I was afraid I would run out of gas because I had been out there for hours. I prayed, 'Papa if You do exist, send me some help.' Within a couple of minutes, I saw lights coming. As I climbed up to the road, I saw it was a white truck. I waved at the driver, and he waved to me to return to my car. I got into my car and buckled up. I saw the man place the tow rope under my car, and he was back in his truck very quickly. I put my car in neutral, and he pulled me out. I put my car in park and unbuckled my seatbelt. By the time I went to get out of my car, he was gone."

Joseph paused as he remembered that day. Timothy was surprised, "What? What did you say?" Joseph asked, "About the guy?" Timothy asked again, "Did you say he was gone? Like, disappeared? Were there tracks?" Joseph continued, "No man. No tracks other than my tracks pulled out of the ditch." Timothy almost shouted, "That is awesome! Did you see the man's face?" Joseph answered, "All I remember was that the truck was white, and I saw his hand. I believe that was an angel." Timothy quickly responded, "Well, yeah! You still didn't believe after that?" Joseph admitted, "I should have, but I was still angry at Papa for taking my mom. When I was little, I used to pray and cry, and I just got angry with Him. I was asking Him to make my dad stop drinking. He never did stop. I stopped praying altogether. I did not believe He was real. I did not believe He cared about me. I believed all the lies."

"What about you? When did you stop believing?" Joseph asked. Timothy thought a moment, "I guess it was in high school. I was so busy thinking that my sister was big stuff, and I wanted to be like her. I thought I was self-made. I never stopped to think about all the favor we had. We went to church, but I never listened to the sermon. Instead, I drifted off into my thoughts. I would stand when everyone else did but had no idea why we were standing. I used to be in my world. Inventing games and picturing different strategies for video games. Sometimes I could hear new songs and see the music notes."

Joseph responded, "I believe that many kids zone out all the time. There is so much happening around them. Do you think video games numb the users?" Timothy replied, "Well, as someone who develops and designs the games. I want to take kids to places they may never be able to experience." Joseph asked again, "Does it numb them?" Timothy continued, "Well, I guess so. I never thought about it that way. I guess if they constantly see killings, it could become the norm." Joseph asked, "Or if they keep seeing zombies and monsters, how does that affect their imagination?" Timothy did not know how to respond. "I guess I hadn't thought about that. What do you think happens to their brains?" Joseph replied, "I truly don't know, but it's just food for thought."

Joseph said, "If my dad had bought me video games, I probably would have gotten lost in them as difficult a time as I had as a kid. I know I would have lost myself in them. I can tell you the few times I played when I was in high school, I did get lost. My high school sweetheart became invisible when I was playing at her house. I decided after that experience that I wouldn't play again."

Timothy changed the subject, "Speaking of high school sweethearts. What happened between you and Cinderella?" Joseph laughed, "Wow! That is a long story. Are you sure you're up to it?" Timothy replied, "yeah, bro. If you can talk about it."

Joseph smiled, "Of course, I can; it is a sweet, bitter story. We met at our freshman year. She was so full of life, and I was sucked dry. As she used to tell it, she saw me sitting alone. I looked like a lost puppy. My side of the story, I sat alone so she would notice me. I had my eyes on her from the moment I first saw her. In algebra class, I could tell she completely understood the lesson. I, on the other hand, had no clue. The day she came over to me, I had my algebra book out, looking at some equations. I was trying to figure out the problem when she walked up and asked if I needed help. I looked up and saw an angel. She was the most beautiful girl I had ever met. Her eyes mesmerized me. They were bluish green. Her smile was bright, and her teeth were the straightest I had ever seen."

Joseph chuckled, "Cyndy was, well, still is beautiful. She sat down to help me. Cyndy explained things better than the teacher did, in my unbiased opinion. I understood the equations the moment she spoke. I know what you must be thinking, but I was not playing dumb. Cyndy did offer me lots of help, but we became good friends first. Then, against the advice of her family, friends, and teachers, she continued to hang out with me. I did not have much of a home life, and she was all about family. Her dad didn't seem to mind me, but her mom disapproved."

Timothy nodded, "Man, that sucks! It makes it rough on a relationship when one or both parents do not approve." Joseph chuckled, "It does, but nothing seems to keep you apart when you are young and in love. We started dating in our sophomore year. Her dad was cool, but her mom gave me the business constantly. She was always asking about my dad. I could not tell her he had passed away. I never really gave her a straight answer. Cyndy would always ask her to drop it, but she wouldn't until her husband stepped in."

Timothy shook his head, "What did your dad have to do with anything?" Joseph replied, "Well, parents want to keep their kids safe. I understand. We dated all through high school. Our senior year, I was looking at going as far as possible from home, and she wanted to stay close to home. I knew I did not want to stick around. We tried a long-distance relationship during our first year in college, but it was too difficult. I wanted her to come to visit, and she wanted me to come home. I was so busy that I finally told her I never wanted to return. That was enough to force her into a decision. I regretted that for many years. The first summer I returned home, I saw her, and she turned and left crying. It bothered me, but I was not planning to return if I did not have to. I never saw her again. If she saw me, I am guessing she must have turned and gone the other way. I looked for her every time I could but never saw her again. I still think about her occasionally. She was my best and only friend. I pretty much have kept my distance from most people. That is, until a month ago."

Joseph was in deep thought. Timothy finally asked, "Well, do you want to see her again?" Joseph responded, "For my sake, yes, but not if I will make her cry. I do not know if she is okay after all this time. I want her to be. I know I broke her heart. I am sure her mother must hate me. I have thought about calling her a few times, but I always chicken out." Timothy asked, "What would it hurt? What is the worst that can happen? She doesn't answer the phone?" Joseph thought for a moment, "Yeah, you're right. I will have to reach out to her; I have so much to share with her. She was my best friend. I did think of her as my best friend for a long time; I still do."

Just then, Lucy returned. Timothy smiled and asked, "Lucy, would you mind if I ask you something?" Lucy looked at Timothy, "Sure, I guess. How may I help you?" Timothy chuckled, "Please don't think me forward. Are you seeing anyone?" Lucy looked at him puzzled, "I'm sorry. I don't feel comfortable answering you." Lucy glanced at Joseph, who was reading something. Timothy quickly replied, "Oh, it's not for me." Lucy replied, "Sir, again, I am not at liberty to discuss my personal affairs with you or any other passenger."

Joseph looked up and spoke, "Lucy, please forgive my new friend Timothy. It seems he is trying to set me up. I thank you for all that you have done for us. Timothy, drop this." Lucy smiled at Joseph, "Well, I can see why he likes you. You are a gentleman." Lucy looked very sternly at Timothy, "While you are here in first class, I can still have you removed. I would appreciate it if you would behave in a gentleman's manner." She glanced back at Joseph, "Gentlemen, please enjoy the rest of your flight. I am available if you need anything. We should be landing soon." Lucy walked away.

Chapter 8 The Pregnant Belly

Joseph had closed his eyes for a nap before landing. Suddenly he heard the captain's voice announcing that they would be arriving at LAX on time. Joseph thought to himself, 'this is the quickest a flight has gone for me. Yah, thank you!' Joseph opened his eyes, expecting to see Timothy sitting next to him. Instead, the seat was empty; he smiled to himself and closed his eyes.

Joseph started to see a movie play before him. He saw his birth mother walking, and she was crying. As she walked, he could see her pregnant belly. She was holding her stomach as if it were heavy. Suddenly she bent over; she looked like she was in great pain. She stumbled and reached for the wall. She leaned against the wall and cried. After some time, she continued to walk. Then she saw a building and started to walk toward it but changed her mind. As she passed the building, he saw the sign. It said abortion clinic. She spoke softly, 'I will not kill you. I am all alone in this, but I will not kill you, baby. I am so afraid for you and me. My parents do not know. I was afraid to tell them because I did not know who the father was. I am so sorry I have failed you. I wish I could love you, but I cannot. I want to, but I am afraid.' Then she started having pain again and walked into the next building. His mother looked around, saw the bathrooms, and headed into the bathroom. She opened the stall door and walked in; she cried. Suddenly she doubled over in tremendous pain. Suddenly she screamed; there was no one to help her, she was alone. She was going to have the baby. In a strange place and all alone, she was panicking. Then she heard a voice, 'Do not fear. Stay calm. I am with you.' She looked around but did not see anyone. She called out, 'Hello. I need help. Can you help me?' She heard the same voice,

'Stay calm. I am with you.' She started to cry, 'Who are you? Where are you?'

Joseph could see and hear everything as if the movie was playing right on a TV screen. She asked again, 'Who are you?' The voice responded, 'I am Yoceph's protector - his guardian angel. She looked around but could not see anyone. The voice spoke again, 'Sit on the floor.' She obeyed, feeling much more at peace. The voice spoke again, 'Do not be afraid. Yoceph is coming soon.' She sat on the floor, quietly she asked, 'Will my baby be, okay?' The voice responded, 'Yes, he will be safe. A man will find him and call for help, and then a couple that needs a baby will adopt him. His new mother will love and care for him. Follow my instructions.' She answered, 'Thank you.'

Joseph suddenly felt so much compassion for his birth mother. He understood that she did not seem to have many options in her life. Joseph also realized that this was part of his story written long before being created. He opened his eyes and saw that Timothy was back in his seat. Joseph closed his eyes again, and the vision continued. He saw this mother in labor. The voice was giving instructions, 'Don't forget to breathe. Push. Push. Push.' Then Joseph saw himself come into the world. He saw that he was so tiny. His mother gently picked him up.

The girl heard the voice say, 'Take your blouse and wipe him clean; wrap the baby in your scarf and place him in your letterman's jacket.' She followed the instruction. Then the voice spoke again, 'Hold Yoceph, close to you. He is very cold.' She picked him up and held him close to her chest. She started to cry. 'You are such a beautiful baby. I am sorry I cannot keep you. I do love you. I will never forget you.' Then she heard the voice again, 'Hurry. You do not want to miss this opportunity.' She hurried out of the building and around the corner. She saw a trash bin and gently placed the baby in the bin. She cried as she walked away; she went into the building and ran up the stairs. She ran to the roof and stood to look down. She could see the trash bin. She heard the trash truck coming. She watched as the man paused before connecting the bin to the truck. He lifted the lid and looked inside. He reached for the varsity athlete's jacket, and a baby fell out.

He yelled to his partner. 'Hold on! Call 911.' He reached in and grabbed the baby and jacket. He wrapped the coat around the baby. He unzipped his jacket and placed the baby close to himself.

Then Joseph looked at his birth mother. She was crying, and he could see a sense of relief. She turned, ran away, and heard the sirens of the police car and ambulance. Joseph saw the ambulance leave with him in it.

Joseph opened his eyes. He thought, 'Wow! I cannot have any doubt that my life was planned long before I thought it was. Thank you, Yah, for showing me this part of my story. I could not have made up such a loving story.'

Timothy stirred and looked over at Joseph, "I just had a weird dream." Joseph chuckled, "Oh really? Do you want to share?" Timothy smiled, "Of course I do. I think this dream was about you." Joseph looked at him, "Really? Do tell."

Timothy began, "I saw this young girl. Maybe high school age. She was pregnant, walked along a sidewalk, and appeared to be on a mission. She was looking for a specific building. However, when she saw it, she immediately changed her mind. I thought the building said abortion or adoption; I could not make out the name. I saw the name at a glance; she was crying and in pain. I could see her face, the anguish she felt. She was, is quite beautiful. I can see your eyes are like hers. She walked by the building, and shortly after, she doubled over in pain. She leaned against a building. After a short time, she walked a little further and walked into a different building. She went straight into the women's restroom. I saw that she was coming out with a baby in her arms, which I presume was you. She had him in her varsity athlete's jacket. She was holding you tightly. She was afraid of dropping you; she walked as if someone was instructing her. She walked to a garbage bin and gently placed the baby inside. She was crying and said, 'I do love you. I am so sorry I can't keep you.' Then she gently placed the baby on the pile of boxes. She walked away crying and ran into the building where she had just exited. She ran upstairs to the roof. From a distance, she watched as a garbage truck drove up."

Timothy continued, "I could hear her saying, 'Please find him. Do not take the trash without looking inside. Please find him. I will scream if they do not look inside first. Please rescue my baby.' She saw the man reach in and pick up the jacket. She had a huge sense of relief as she watched the man pick up the baby and warm him with his body. She started to cry. She turned and ran away. She was afraid to be found." Timothy looked at Joseph and asked, "Well? Do you think this is about you?" Joseph quietly said, "That's a confirmation. Will you believe me if I tell you I had just had a vision with everything almost exactly the way you dreamt it?"

Timothy was amazed, "I can tell you that I will believe almost anything after this flight. This flight has been the most memorable, supernatural, and eye-opening flight or even experience I have ever had. I had never felt like this before or dreamt like this either. I believe! I do believe in the All Mighty God."

As the men were finishing their conversation, they heard the pilot ask the flight attendants to prepare for landing.

Joseph smiled at Timothy, "It has been an amazing flight. Timothy, I look forward to our next visit. Here's my card." Joseph handed Timothy his card; it was almost plain-looking. It was white, with red lettering. It read Joseph Warrior of Yahushuah HaMashiach. Timothy smiled, "I don't even know your last name, but I feel I have known you all my life." Joseph smiled, "Well, I was adopted into the Arias family, but Yah is my Father. So, legally in the natural, that is my last name."

"Let's make a plan to get together soon. May I call you if I am struggling at the funeral?" Timothy asked. Joseph answered, "Yes, of course. Let's exchange numbers so I know you are calling me." The men exchanged information.

Lucy walked up, checking on the seatbelts. "Gentlemen, it has been a pleasure serving you today. I do hope we meet again." She smiled at Joseph and walked away. Timothy jumped at the opportunity, "Dude, you gotta get her phone number. I think she is sweet on you." Joseph smiled, "If it is meant to be, we will meet again." Joseph rested his head back and began to reflect on the day's events.

Joseph glanced over at his new friend, that seemed like an old friend. He smiled to himself as he thought, 'Maybe this is what it feels like to have a brother.' He looked over at Timothy, "Maybe I can rearrange my schedule and join you at your family's home. Do you think that would be okay?" Timothy was pleasantly surprised, "That would be so cool, dude. My sister will love you! So will my niece." Joseph laughed, "Don't get too excited yet. I must make several calls to see if I can reschedule or rearrange them. Do you know the day of the funeral?"

Timothy shook his head, "No. Sorry, when I heard mom died, I did not hear much else. I can find out as soon as we land." Joseph nodded his head, "Okay. That sounds fine; I will send my assistant an email before we land and get the ball rolling. I will most likely still need to keep my business dinner dates." Joseph asked, "I forgot to ask where your mom lived?" Timothy answered, "Her house is in a neighborhood called Diamond Bar. It is a nice area. Pretty quiet." Joseph smiled, "That's not too far from my house; I live in Manhattan Beach. It is a beach town and a very laid-back community. It is a cool place to be. Much better than the Mid-West where I grew up."

"Mid-West?" Timothy asked. "Yep!" Joseph chuckled. Timothy responded, "I guess we can talk about that another time." Joseph replied, "Yeah, that's an extremely long story. Where did you end up living?" Timothy laughed, "Well, you can say that I am a gypsy. I do not have a home; I go wherever the business sends me. I tend to live out of my suitcase. Wherever my assignments are, I have a home, or an apartment fully furnished and a car. The longest time I have stayed in one place is six months. I was in London for four weeks when the call came. My work there is incomplete, so I will have to return afterward." Joseph asked, "Do you usually know how long you will be at any place?" Timothy replied, "No, I arrive and start working. I do not have much of a life. That's why I develop games in my spare time."

Rachel Velasquez

Psalm 139:13-18

For You formed my innermost parts;
You knit me [together] in my mother's womb.
I will give thanks and praise to You, for I am fearfully and
wonderfully made;
Wonderful are Your works,
And my soul knows it very well.
My frame was not hidden from You,
When I was being formed in secret,
And intricately and skillfully formed [as if embroidered with many
colors] in the depths of the earth.
Your eyes have seen my unformed substance;
And in Your book were all written
The days that were appointed for me,
When as yet there was not one of them [even taking shape].
How precious also are Your thoughts to me, O God!
How vast is the sum of them!
If I could count them, they would outnumber the sand.
When I awake, I am still with You.

Chapter 9 The Beach

Joseph's phone rang as his feet hit the ground. "Hello, Samantha. How are you?" Samantha replied, "You always surprise me by asking how I am doing. Most people I have worked for are all business. Sir." Joseph interrupted, "Please call me Joseph. Sir would be an older guy." Samantha continued, "Joseph, I am doing well. Thank you for asking. I made all the appropriate calls, and the only dinner I could not reschedule was with Mr. Jones. He insisted on meeting with you. However, he said he was willing to come to you, wherever you may be."

Joseph chuckled, "Thank you, Samantha. Can you call Mr. Jones and ask if he can meet me tonight at my place?" Samantha responded, "I will be happy to ask him. What time is good for you?" Joseph replied, "I need an hour and a half to get home and clean up. Any time after that would be great, also as late as I need, works for me too. I will leave my home tomorrow morning, and you will be able to reach me by text." Samantha replied, "Joseph, welcome home. I will let him know and will get back to you soon. Do you want me to give him directions to you, or do you want to forward him directions?" Joseph answered, "Please give him my number and tell him to call me. You can have the rest of the week off, paid, of course." Samantha replied, "Thank you! Please call me if I can be of some assistance for this event you are attending." Joseph replied, "Thank you for offering, but I just gave you the week off. Enjoy!"

Joseph walked towards Timothy. "Would you like a ride, or is someone coming to pick you up?" Timothy replied, "I was going to see if they had a rental car available." Joseph added, "If you don't mind waiting to get to your sister's until tomorrow. You are welcome to crash at my place tonight, and I will join you tomorrow. I do have a business meeting coming tonight."

Timothy smiled, "Do you want me to join in the meeting?" Joseph grinned, "If you would like to. Mr. Jones is coming to the house, and you are a guest of mine." Timothy answered, "Well, I guess I better clean up before your guest arrives." Joseph replied, "I believe we will have plenty of time. Let's get our bags."

As the men walked out and down to baggage, Joseph attempted to prepare Timothy for his home. "I hope you like the ocean. I have a flat by the beach; it's the upper level of a two-story home. It is very relaxing. I thought it would be good for you to get some rest before heading to your sister's house. Did you plan on staying with Karen?" Timothy replied, "Honestly, I had not made any plans." Joseph answered, "Well, you are welcome to stay here, but if you decide to stay in Diamond Bar after seeing your siblings, that works too. So, I am giving you another option." Timothy smiled, "Thanks, dude. I truly appreciate it."

Joseph asked, "How are you going to explain me to your siblings?" Timothy answered jokingly, "I will tell them I adopted you." Joseph laughed, "I guess I better act like a little child. Shall I throw a tantrum?" Timothy laughed, "I would like to see that."

After getting their luggage, Joseph headed toward his car. "Do you always park your car here?" Timothy asked. Joseph replied, "No. Only when I know I am not gone more than a couple of weeks. After that, I will usually Uber, or on occasion, my assistant Samantha offers to drop me off." Timothy chuckled, "Looks like we both travel light." Joseph smiled, "I don't have too much with me. I tend to buy whatever I need once I arrive. I also enjoy donating what I buy." Timothy responded, "Me too."

The men walked toward a puke green, older car. Timothy was the first to speak, "Is that your car?" Joseph answered, "Yeah. What do you think?" Timothy laughed, "I think my grandpa had one of these." Joseph replied, "It was the only car I could afford when I went to college. I bought it with my own money for $100. I learned to work on it and ended up restoring it. It was one huge rust bucket when I got it." Timothy asked, "Why did you keep it once you made money?" Joseph replied, "I wanted to have something I owned to hand down to my children one day."

Timothy was walking around the car. "I can't believe you have one of these. What year is it?" Joseph smiled, "1966." Timothy continued, "Chevy II. I always hoped that I could have been able to keep my grandpa's car. I think dad sold it when grandpa died. I didn't have a choice in the matter." Joseph laughed, "Well, maybe this is the one. I know that a taxi company in San Diego had a bunch." Timothy smiled, "My last memory of my grandpa was him driving up to our house in his Chevy II. He would sing a little tune. It was quite catchy. Let's count down, Timmy boy! Ten then nine, put them in a line. Eight then seven, my name is Grandpa Kevin. Six then five, I am still alive! Four then three, quiet as a honeybee. Two just like my Chevy II. One, now you have won. He would then proceed to give me a lollypop."

Joseph was unlocking his car and putting his luggage in the trunk. "That's a cool memory. I do not remember if I ever met my grandparents. Come on, let's head out." Timothy put his luggage into the trunk.

"I live about 20-30 minutes away depending on traffic. Are you hungry?" Joseph asked. Timothy replied, "Yeah, I could eat something." Joseph replied, "Samantha most likely stocked my refrigerator yesterday, but we can also grab a bite at any of the local places. What do you feel like?" Timothy chuckled, "I could go for a shower first." Joseph replied with a smile, "I have one of those at home."

"You know, growing up, I didn't make it to the beach very often. Mom was terrified of sharks. She thought the sharks were lurking in the water, ready to enjoy a little bite out of me." Timothy chuckled. Joseph added, "I guess she just wanted to keep you safe." Timothy replied, "Yeah, that kind of put the fear of God in me, so I didn't swim in the ocean much. I got away a couple of times with friends but did not go further than waist deep. I realize I missed out on a bunch of fun." Joseph added, "I'm sure you did, but you also didn't get attacked by a shark, right?"

Timothy laughed, "Yeah, I guess you're right. Mom kept me safe." Joseph laughed, "Well, she isn't here now, so if you want to go into the ocean, I also have a wetsuit that should fit you." Timothy looked surprised, "What? You want me to go in the ocean?" Joseph pushed, "Are you afraid?" Timothy shook his head, "Not really. I don't think I should." Joseph replied, "If you aren't afraid, we can do some surfing. I will teach you." Timothy chuckled, "Well, I have complete faith that you would keep me safe. Okay, let's do it."

Joseph smiled, "Perfect, let me check my schedule so we can plan." Timothy asked, "Are you serious?" Joseph smiled, "Of course I am. It feels like no one else is on earth when you are on the ocean. There is a calm in the storm of the waves." Timothy asked, "How long have you been surfing?" Joseph answered, "When I came down to college I met a guy in my first class, and after class, he was on his way to surf. One conversation led to another, and he taught me to surf."

Timothy laughed, "I can see that happening. Just like you and me." Joseph laughed. "Well, here we are." Timothy was amazed, "Wow! This view is amazing. I can't believe people live on the beach." Joseph answered, "Well, I am not actually on the beach. There is a walkway between my place and the ocean.

As the men entered the house, Timothy walked straight to the front of the house. He gazed out, "Dude, I can't believe your view. It is amazing." Joseph laughed, "Yeah, it is relaxing. It helps me calm down after a long day at work."

Timothy turned to face Joseph, "I would love to live here. The location is out of this world." Joseph smiled, "Well, when I got the place, I wasn't sure I could live here because it was so quiet. It brought back too many memories that were not very pleasant. But, as the days went by, the memories faded. So, it has become a respite." Timothy added, "I can see how. Thanks for inviting me. I needed this peaceful quiet before heading to my sister's tomorrow."

Joseph added, "Well, the guest bedroom and bath are to your left. You will enjoy the view. Not as good as the front, but you can still see the ocean." Timothy grabbed his luggage and walked into the guest room. Joseph had the sliding doors open with the curtains pulled back. Timothy smiled as he saw the ocean in front of him. Timothy dropped his luggage on the bed and walked onto the patio. Timothy took a deep breath; he realized how much he missed home as he breathed in the fresh air. He heard the waves gently rolling in. It sounded as though he was standing in the water, loud and overpowering." Suddenly he heard Joseph, "I could stay out here all night." Timothy turned to face Joseph, "Do you sleep out here?" Joseph responded, "Not as much as I used to when I first moved in. I used to fall asleep in my recliner. The sound of the waves just knocked me out." Timothy replied, "Would it be okay if I slept out here instead of the bed?"

Joseph smiled, "Of course. Make yourself at home. I will jump in the shower and get ready for my meeting. Do you want to go out for dinner or stay in?" Timothy answered, "I think I want to stay in." Joseph replied, "Sounds good to me. I am sure I have some salad. I will look and see what kind of fish I have. I'll throw it in the oven and then clean up."

Timothy was enjoying the view and lost in his thoughts. He remembered the first time he came out to the ocean without his mom's consent. He had been too afraid to go into the water. The ringing of his phone startled him. "Hello, Karen. How are you?" Karen asked, "When do you land? I was hoping to come to pick you up, so you don't have to get a car." Timothy responded, "I don't want to put you out. I will have a friend bring me by tomorrow." Karen did not sound happy, "You don't want me to pick you up?" Timothy answered, "Karen, I will be at your house in the morning. What time is a good time for me to arrive?" Karen replied, "As soon as you land." Timothy answered, "My friend Joseph is going to host me tonight. I hope that is okay." Karen replied, "Tim, I haven't seen you in ages and need to see you." Timothy responded, "Sis. I will be at your house in the morning. Text me your address so I can get directions." Karen asked, "Tim? Are you already in town?"

Timothy felt uncomfortable, "Sis, I love you, but I am not a little kid anymore. I will see you in the morning. I will have my friend Joseph with me." Karen replied, "Timmie? I love you. You know I am not angry with you, right?" Timothy responded, "Yes, I know. Listen, Karen. I love you; however, I need tonight to chill out before facing the others. I hope you can understand." Karen responded, "It's okay. Take your time. We will see you tomorrow. Timmie Rae is excited to see you. She has been asking about you all day." Timothy quietly replied, "I can't wait to see her. Tell her that I will be there early, maybe about 9:30. Why don't you tell her at 10:00 to be safe?"

Joseph had stepped into his kitchen and was pulling out salad and fish. He prepared the salmon with lemon and seasonings and wrapped it up and threw it in the oven. He pulled out the lettuce and dumped it into a salad bowl and turned to head into his room when he heard a text come through. Joseph smiled to himself and responded to the text, 'Samantha, please forgive me if I have not told you this. You are the best! Thanks for the salmon and salad.' Samantha responded, 'I also made you some homemade mashed potatoes just in case you'd like that. You must microwave it for a few minutes or throw it in the oven. You will find mangoes and avocado on your counter. Have a good night.' He responded, 'You really are the best! Thanks for all you do for me. I will talk to you tomorrow if I need anything. Have a good night.'

Joseph walked into his bedroom and headed to the shower. As he showered, he thought about his meeting with Mr. Jones. 'Wonder why Mr. Jones is so eager to meet?' As he exited the shower, he heard a text. He reached for his cell and saw it was Mr. Jones. 'I am in your area early. Is it okay if I come early?' Joseph responded, 'Of course! You can have dinner here with my friend and me.' Mr. Jones replied, "Oh no, I didn't mean to interrupt your dinner plans.' Joseph opted to dial Mr. Jones. "Hello, Joseph." Joseph smiled, "Mr. Jones, please honor me by joining us for dinner. Besides, I have so much food, thanks to my assistant Samantha." Mr. Jones replied, "Well, if you insist. May I bring over some wine?" Joseph answered, "Yes, of course. What time will you arrive?" Mr. Jones laughed, "I am at your door now." Joseph laughed, "Give me a minute. I am just getting out of the shower." Mr. Jones laughed, "I can wait at the beach while you get ready." Joseph answered, "No, no. Please do not do that. I am walking to the door now."

Joseph reached for the doorknob as he hollered for Timothy, "My meeting has arrived early." He opened the door and greeted Mr. Jones, "Thank you for coming here. It made my life so much easier. Please come in, and please excuse my attire." Mr. Jones laughed and jokingly said, "I am glad to see that you have clothes on." Again, Joseph laughed, "Would you feel more comfortable without your jacket?" Mr. Jones was removing his jacket and untying his tie. "Yes, thank you."

Joseph led him into the living room. You are welcome to enjoy the view as I finish dinner. Mr. Jones smiled, "I am impressed with this beautiful view, but I am handy in the kitchen, so don't feel that you must entertain me." Joseph smiled, "I need to make sure my friend heard me when I hollered that you had arrived early." Next, Joseph knocked on Timothy's door, "Timothy, Mr. Jones has arrived; dress casually; we will hang out." Timothy replied, "Okay, I will be out in a few minutes."

Mr. Jones stood looking out, "Joseph, I see why you are so calm; your home feels so peaceful." Joseph responded, "Yes, most people seem to be at peace here. It is a friendly neighborhood. My neighbors look out for my place when I travel. My assistant Samantha also comes over quite often while I am away." Mr. Jones turned to face Joseph, "Yes, Samantha takes excellent care of your time. She was like a pit bull when it came to your time. I had to be very persistent." Joseph laughed, "Yes. She takes good care of my time. She knows the importance of rest. I have given her time off and told her not to reply to anyone calling her cell. I will take a little time off, which means she is off too."

Mr. Jones asked, "If I am not too forward, what will you do with your time off?" Joseph smiled, "I will be helping a friend. I hope that I will also have time to surf. I try to surf as often as I can." Mr. Jones added, "That is a good policy to have. Time off is a necessity. What else do you enjoy for recreation?" Joseph laughed, "If I told you, I'm afraid you wouldn't believe me." Mr. Jones laughed, "Try me."

Timothy entered the kitchen, "I hope I am not changing the subject, but what are we having for dinner? Smells delicious." Joseph smiled, "Timothy, this is Mr. Jones. Mr. Jones, this is Timothy, my new friend and brother." Mr. Jones looked confused, "New friend? Brother?" Timothy laughed, "Yes, we just met on the flight home from Europe. Brother because we hit it off, and our newfound friendship is more like one of the brothers." Mr. Jones smiled, "Yes, yes. I see. There are not too many people like that nowadays."

Mr. Jones watched as Joseph pulled out a dish from the refrigerator and placed it in the oven. "What is on the menu tonight?" Joseph smiled and, with a laugh, said, "Well, I have salad…yum! Salmon and taters. I am also going to make mango avocado salsa." Timothy answered before Mr. Jones, "That sounds delicious!" Mr. Jones chimed in, "It does sound fantastic. May I help with anything?" Joseph replied, "Well, if you men will set the table. Everything you will need is in that cupboard. I can handle the rest." He pointed across the kitchen.

Mr. Jones went to the living room and grabbed the wine. "I brought some Chardonnay. That'll be a perfect pairing." He walked into the kitchen, "Where do you have your corkscrew?" Joseph smiled, "Honestly, I am not much of a wine drinker, so I don't believe I have one." When I asked her, Mr. Jones answered, "Samantha thought you would like a white wine." Joseph laughed, "Maybe she brought one? She thinks of everything." Mr. Jones laughed, "Okay, I will look! Do you have wine glasses?" Joseph laughed as he pointed, "Look right above you in that cabinet." Mr. Jones opened the cabinet and found everything he needed. Mr. Jones said, "You need to give that young lady a raise." Joseph laughed, "Yes, I do!" Mr. Jones and Timothy set the table and laughed as they began to guess what Samantha's appearance must be. Joseph would shake his head as they asked. "Does she have brown hair?" Timothy asked. Joseph responded, "No." Mr. Jones asked, "Is she a redhead?" Joseph laughed, "No." Timothy asked, "Is she a blonde?" "No." Joseph laughed.

Mr. Jones asked, "She must have black hair." Joseph laughed so loudly that the men turned to face him, "No!" "Well, what color is her hair?" Timothy asked. Joseph was laughing so hard he could hardly speak, "Believe it or not, she wears her hair a dark blue. When I first met her, she had dark brown hair. She asked me if I would mind if she changed her hair color. I expected her to go blonde or light brown, but I thought it was black when I first saw her. It looks good on her. She is extremely professional."

Timothy laughed and asked, "Can we continue our guessing?" Joseph smiled, "I think that's enough for tonight. She is such an excellent assistant. I want to keep it professional for us both."

Joseph had finished the salsa as the men finished setting the table. "Well, it looks like dinner is ready. I will bring the food to the table. Timothy, can you check the pantry for some bread." Joseph pointed. Timothy answered, "Looks like Samantha gets extra points. She has a loaf of freshly baked bread."

Joseph asked Mr. Jones, "Do you mind if I say grace?" Mr. Jones smiled, "I would like that." Joseph smiled and began, "Heavenly Father, I thank you for your presence and this time with friends. Bless this meal, our time together, and Samantha. Please join us as we nourish our bodies. In the Name of Your Son, Yahushuah HaMashiach. Amen."

Mr. Jones stated, "You know, I am blessed that you have invited me to dinner, even though I pushed my way in." Joseph smiled, "I am glad you are here, Mr. Jones." Mr. Jones responded, "Please call me Paul." Joseph replied, "As you wish, Paul." Timothy added, "Mr. Jones, I must admit that I felt uncomfortable coming out when I heard you were early. I didn't want to infringe on your meeting." Mr. Jones responded, "Timothy, please call me Paul as well. Why would you feel uncomfortable?" Timothy replied, "Well, my trip here to Joseph's was unplanned. It just evolved on the plane." Suddenly Mr. Jones started to laugh, "Oh my! This dinner is heavenly!" Timothy and Joseph looked at each other and smiled.

Mr. Jones laughed, "I have never tasted anything so delicious; what is your secret ingredient?" Joseph smiled, "I believe what you are experiencing is the presence of the Lord. Remember I invited him to dinner." Timothy nodded his head, "This does taste amazing." Joseph added, "Can you smell His presence?" Mr. Jones said, "Maybe that's what's going on with the food. Joseph, I am a believer. I just knew I had to meet with you tonight. I felt an urgency from the Lord." Joseph asked, "Do you know why?" Mr. Jones responded, "No, I don't. I was thinking about waiting until after your trip but felt I should not. Is there something I should know about your business?"

Joseph smiled, "Shall we wait to speak about business until after dinner. Let's enjoy the Lord's presence and commune with Him." Mr. Jones added, "Well, aside from this being the most delicious meal I have ever tasted. I can't get over the view you have." Timothy asked, "Paul, do you live in town?" Mr. Jones replied, "No. I traveled here by car this morning for this meeting. I am from Phoenix. I have not even gotten a hotel room yet. I was considering driving home afterward." Joseph looked at him, "Paul, please do not even entertain that thought. You are welcome to crash here for the night. Mi casa es tu casa." Timothy added, "You are welcome to sleep in the guest room. I plan to sleep outdoors on the deck." Mr. Jones looked down, "Please do not think I planned to crash here and especially kick you out of a bed you've been invited to stay at."

Joseph answered, "I have a blow-up mattress, so no one needs to be on the couch or floor." Timothy laughed, "I was just going to sleep on the recliner outside." Joseph laughed, "I didn't think you were serious. It gets chilly out here at night." Mr. Jones smiled, "I accept your invitation. I have never slept at the beach, so this is a new experience." Timothy laughed, "That makes two of us." Joseph smiled, "Well, if either one of you wants to surf, I will be up early. You're welcome to join me." Mr. Jones replied, "It depends on how late we go to bed." Joseph replied, "I surf regardless of how little sleep I get. I am not home as much as I would like to be, so I take advantage of every opportunity." Timothy answered, "Not me. I need my beauty sleep. Besides, I need to rest up to face the family."

When the men finished the meal, Joseph grabbed some bread. He looked at the men. "When Jesus/Yahushuah walked on earth as the Son of Man, his final days before He gave His life for us, the feast of Unleavened Bread was fast approaching. The priests were looking for a way to execute Yahushuah. They schemed and made their plans. He sent two of His disciples to prepare a place to eat the Passover dinner. Everything He told the disciples took place just as He had said. When the hour came to eat, they sat, and He told them that He earnestly wanted to eat this Passover meal with them before He suffered. Then after dinner, He gave thanks for the cup and asked them to pass it around for them to share. He asked his disciples to remember Him. He told them that the 'bread is My body, which will be broken for you'. Then He gave thanks for the cup and said, "This cup, which is poured out for you, is the renewed covenant of My blood." So today, YHVH, we thank You for this bread that is Your body and this drink that is Your blood for the new covenant. Thank You for Your sacrifice of the Innocent Lamb, Your Son, and my Savior. Yahushuah HaMashiach. Thank you. Do eat and drink." The men had a few minutes of silence as they thanked and enjoyed personal time with the Lord.

Joseph was the first to speak. "Shall we continue our discussion in the living room?" Mr. Jones smiled, "Yes, that would be fine." However, Timothy insisted, "While you two discuss business, I will care for the dishes." Joseph attempted to argue, "You are my guest. Please leave them; I will take care of it later." Timothy replied, "This is the least I can do. Please enjoy your discussion."

Joseph and Mr. Jones walked to the living room. Mr. Jones spoke first, "Joseph, I want to hire you to come and speak at my office in Phoenlx. Do training or whatever you see fit. I have 300 employees, and they need to hear from you. I know you have a message for them." Joseph asked, "Why me? What do you expect?" Mr. Jones answered, "I honestly do not know. I was praying one day, and my computer turned on right to your website. I reviewed it and prayed some more. Finally, I felt in my spirit that you are the one I need."

Joseph asked, "What is going on with your employees?" Mr. Jones replied, "I feel a dark presence over them. Production has dropped significantly, and my management team is at a loss." Joseph encouraged him, "Tell me more." Mr. Jones replied, "I have sent teams to team-building retreats, and nothing has come from that. I do not want to fire people; however, I am so close to starting over with a completely new team. Management wants to fire almost everyone. I want to avoid that if possible. Most of my employees have been with me since the start of my business. They are family to me, and I care about them all." Joseph could hear and feel his heart, "I will have to pray and see what the Lord says to me. I do not move unless he tells me to." Mr. Jones smiled, "I believe that is a yes." Joseph smiled and said, "I must pray about it. I understand that you heard that it was me, but I must hear for myself." Mr. Jones smiled, "Tell me what you feel now." Joseph smiled, "I don't want to give you a false sense, so I will wait to hear then give you an answer. If I hear yes, what is your availability?" Mr. Jones smiled, "Tomorrow."

Joseph smiled, "Okay. As soon as I hear, I will make the proper arrangements. I am on vacation for two weeks and then have prior assignments. Samantha oversees my schedule. I will reach out to you first to confirm yea or nay. Samantha is the person that will get the ball rolling. As far as my compensation." Mr. Jones interrupted, "I will pay you whatever I need to. I will even double your fee if you make me a priority. I believe it is life or death for my business. That is why I drove out here. I needed to make sure you met with me." Joseph asked, "Is there anything else I need to know about your business?" Mr. Jones asked, "Like what? I will give you anything you may need. Reports?" Joseph responded, "It is okay. I usually get some revelation before I come out to visit a site. My first visit is normally a week; then, I return after two weeks. At that time, I know how much time I will need to spend with clients and teams." Mr. Jones replied, "I know. I read all about your techniques. I know that you carry something no one else seems to. Besides, you come highly recommended by God."

Timothy finished as the two men finished their conversation. "Well, shall we go out for dessert?" Joseph answered, "I will bet you may find something there if you look in my fridge." Timothy laughed and teased, "Shall we take bets?" Joseph laughed, "I can't take your money. I already saw what was in the fridge." Mr. Jones asked, "What is it?" Joseph grinned, "It is my favorite. I believe there should be some ice cream in the freezer for German chocolate cake. I was gone for a few months on my last trip to Europe, and Samantha tends to spoil me when I return." Mr. Jones asked jokingly, "Is she married? It sounds like she may be a good fit for you."

Joseph laughed, "Don't you start too. Timothy has already attempted to set me up with his sister and our flight attendant." Timothy laughed and responded, "In my defense, I want someone great for my sister." The men laughed as they headed into the kitchen to join Timothy and get some dessert. Mr. Jones continued, "The problem is that Samantha doesn't realize that she is doing too much for you. If she continues this way, you will never need a wife." Joseph laughed, "She is like a little sister I never had. She is much too young for me."

Timothy placed the German Chocolate Cake on the counter and turned to get the ice cream out of the fridge. "Oh wow! The freezer is my kind of freezer. What flavor of ice cream would you like? We have vanilla, chocolate, and nutty coconut." Timothy turned to face the men. Mr. Jones smiled from ear to ear, "I would love some chocolate." Joseph smiled shyly, "I will take some nutty coconut." Timothy adds, "Well, I will take a scoop of each."

Joseph grabbed the ice cream scoop and some plates. "I may take a scoop of each, so you don't feel bad, Timothy." Mr. Jones chuckled, "Are you trying to make me join you?" Joseph laughed, "Well? Is it working?" Mr. Jones laughed, "Yes, it is." Timothy replied, "Perfect! Three scoops of ice cream with a slice of cake."

The men headed back to the living room. As they enjoyed their dessert, the conversation shifted to Timothy. Mr. Jones asked, "Timothy, where do you live?" Timothy replied, "Honestly, I am a gypsy. My company moves me around and gives me a place to live and a car to drive." Mr. Jones asked, "Is this your hometown?" Timothy answered, "No. I grew up about an hour and a half from here. I am headed home for my mother's funeral." Mr. Jones replied, "I am sorry to hear about your loss. She was a wonderful mother; I am sure of that. Look how good you turned out." Timothy smiled, "Yes. She was the best."

Joseph saw the pain Timothy was feeling, so he changed the subject. "Well, who will join me surfing in the morning?" Timothy smiled, "I think I will sit on the beach and watch you. I won't go in this time." The men looked at Mr. Jones, who was in deep thought. Joseph asked, "Paul, will you surf tomorrow?" Mr. Jones looked at him and then at Timothy. "Would you consider doing a job change, Timothy?" Timothy was a little surprised by the question, "I had not even thought about changing jobs." Mr. Jones continued, "I would match whatever you make and even offer you a bonus. I am always on the lookout for the right employee." Timothy looked at him, "I don't know. I enjoy what I do." Mr. Jones pressed, "I know I caught you off guard; however, you would be stationary instead of homeless." Timothy smiled, "As tempting as it sounds, I will need to think about this offer. I will think about it, but first, I need to get through the funeral." Mr. Jones added, "Take your time. I would never pressure anyone. I know when I meet someone I truly like. The offer will remain on the table until you decide, and I will leave the offer open." Timothy nodded his head, "I appreciate the offer. I will pray about this."

Joseph smiled, "Well, the wind is picking up outside. I will stand on the deck if you want to join me. No pressure: you are welcome to stay indoors and enjoy the scene from here." He added, "Paul, I can give you a pair of shorts and a t-shirt if you want to get more comfortable. I also have extra pajamas for you. I set them out." Mr. Jones replied, "Joseph, you are the perfect host. Thank you for your kindness." Joseph smiled, "It is my pleasure. I don't have guests too often." Mr. Jones stood up and reached for the dessert plates, "I will take care of these." Timothy answered, "Thank you. I will make room for you in the bedroom."

Joseph headed into his bedroom for the clothes. As he re-entered, "Fortunately, you are about the same size, so these clothes should fit pretty well." Mr. Jones turned to face Joseph, "I think I may be a little chubbier." He laughed. Joseph smiled, "I still think these will fit just fine." Mr. Jones replied, "I appreciate your hospitality. You have made me feel extremely comfortable." Joseph smiled, "We are supposed to open our doors for travelers. I believe you fall into that. Besides, I like you." Mr. Jones smiled, "If I had a son, I would hope that he was just like you; you make me feel so calm." Joseph smiled as he handed the clothes to Mr. Jones.

Joseph changed into his wetsuit and headed out to surf. He lifted his eyes and saw the moon was full and very bright. Joseph knew he would be able to see the waves. As he hit the water, he felt the adrenaline rush. Joseph took a deep breath and dove with his board. As he surfaced, he heard nothing but waves pounding the beach. He paddled out then sat up; he heard complete silence. Joseph looked up and smiled. There was a peace and a calm that he felt out on the ocean all alone. He spoke, "Yah, thank you for this beautiful ocean I get to enjoy. It is beautiful in the day and at night." Joseph looked around and saw the lights of the homes on the beach. He searched the landscape for his home. Then he saw a couple of figures standing on the beach waving. He knew it must be his two new friends. He waved but was not sure they would see him.

The moonlight was bright. Suddenly, Joseph felt it. It was a good wave to take. He started paddling; his arms were swimming when suddenly he jumped up. Joseph laughed. It was a perfect wave. It felt like an eternity, but he knew the wave would not last forever. The rumble of the wave was deafening. He was on top and working his way across the wave. Joseph felt something hit under his board, and it flew out from under his feet. WIPEOUT! He popped out and saw his board. Joseph swam to it and got back on. As he swam out into the dark, he wondered, 'Why do people have a fear of the water? I know there is so much power, but Yahushuah calmed the seas. Can I do that?' Joseph heard a voice say, 'If you calm it now, your surfing time is over.' Joseph laughed. He thought to himself, 'I have guests so I won't stay out too long. Just a few more runs.' Joseph caught a few more waves then headed in.

His new friends were standing on the beach laughing. Timothy yelled, "Dude! That was awesome! I felt like I was out there with you." Joseph answered, "You should have come out." Mr. Jones added, "That looks like so much fun, but I am not a strong swimmer, so I wouldn't be able to join you." Joseph asked, "Do you want to body surf?" Mr. Jones quickly replied, "No. Not me. I could drown. My body does not float well." Timothy agreed, "I don't think my body would float either. Besides, the night puts a little fear in me. I was afraid for you." Joseph chuckled, "I was born to be in the water. I love it." Timothy answered, "I can tell."

Joseph asked, "Do you want to do anything out here? Or are you ready to head in?" Timothy answered first, "I am ready for bed." Mr. Jones agreed, "I am too. It has been a long day." Joseph agreed, "It has been a long day." The men walked to the house. Joseph explained the rush he felt when riding the wave. "I don't know how to explain it, and truly there is a sense of being closer to Yah when I am out there. It is easier for me to hear Him. Riding the waves gives me the feeling of walking on water. It is pretty cool."

Mr. Jones asked, "Don't you have any fear?" Joseph answered, "I was afraid the first few times I surfed but then I just kind of came to an understanding. If it were my turn to go, it would not matter where I was. Whether it was on the ocean, sky, or land; so why worry about it. I know the Lord protects me. I do not push it, though. I only do night surfing when the moonlight is so bright that it allows me to see clearly." As they entered the house, Joseph smiled at Timothy, "Are you still thinking of sleeping on the deck?" Timothy replied, "I think so. Do you think it's too cold out here?"

Joseph replied, "I think it is, but it's up to you. I can set up the blowup mattress, so you have it as an option if it gets too cold during the night." Timothy said, "Thanks, that will work." Joseph added, "You could also sleep inside with the sliding door open, and you will get the same effect." Timothy replied, "I will check that option out too. I know I will fall sound asleep as soon as my head hits the pillow."

Mr. Jones excused himself, "Gentlemen, I will call my wife and go to bed. What time are we planning to wake up?" Joseph looked at

Timothy, "What time do you want to be at your sister's?" Timothy answered, "Between 9:30 and 10." Joseph replied, "Ok. Breakfast would need to be at seven. Gentlemen, have a great night's sleep." Timothy chuckled, "Goodnight, John-boy." Mr. Jones did not skip a beat, "Goodnight, Elizabeth." The men laughed and headed off to bed.

1 Peter 4:8-9

Above all, have fervent and unfailing love for one another,

because love covers a multitude of sins,

it overlooks unkindness and unselfishly seeks the best for others.
Welcome one another into your homes without grumbling.

Chapter 10 Catch a Wave

Joseph had set his alarm for 5:30 am. He wanted to catch a few waves before having breakfast. As his alarm sounded, Joseph jumped up and out of bed. As he dressed, he was in thought about Mr. Jones' proposal. Joseph grabbed his surfboard and jogged out across the sand. He felt the cool sand on his feet and thought about his first time on the sand. Joseph was about eighteen years old. He had flown out to see some of the colleges recruiting him. When he landed, his first request was to go to the beach. Joseph remembered the black suit. When he arrived at the beach, he rolled up his pants to not get them dirty. He could picture himself and thought, 'What a sight I was.' He laughed aloud. He remembered saying, "I am home. I will live here one day." He thought to himself, 'Funny, it came true.'

Joseph jogged into the water. When it became too deep, he dropped his board. As he paddled out, he heard, 'Son, I sent Paul. Go, and I will go out before you. I have prepared this path for you. I will use you to change this business.' Joseph had taken in a few waves when he looked at his watch and decided it was time to head back. He was waiting for a big one. When he heard, 'Go now.' He looked around and started to swim to the shore. He felt the wave and stood up, and it was the best he had caught in a while. It took him almost to the shoreline. Joseph was laughing. As he lifted his eyes to his home, he noticed that Timothy was standing outside watching. He had found the binoculars.

He waved at Timothy. As Joseph jogged home, he knew that breakfast would be fun. It was as if he could hear the conversations. Joseph chuckled to himself. When he was close enough, Timothy yelled, "Dude! I almost want to surf. You make it look so fun and easy!"

Joseph stopped and pretended to hand him the surfboard. Timothy laughed, "Not today! But I will do it after I'm done with the family business."

Joseph was entering the front door when Mr. Jones was exiting the bedroom. Mr. Jones asked, "Did you go surfing this early?" Joseph answered, "I told you I get as much surfing done as possible when home." Mr. Jones shook his head, "Joseph, you are serious about your recreation. I like that! A man that plays hard also works hard." Joseph laughed, "I am hitting the shower, and we will be having breakfast at seven." Mr. Jones had already showered and headed into the kitchen. Timothy headed to the shower.

When Joseph and Timothy exited their bedrooms, they were pleasantly surprised to smell breakfast cooking. Joseph asked, "Paul, did you find everything you needed or wanted? Is there something I can help you with?" Mr. Jones answered, "I have everything under control." Joseph asked again, "What can I get out?" Mr. Jones smiled, "I have everything under control. You have been so gracious to me. The least I can do is make you breakfast; you fixed me dinner and hosted me overnight. Please allow me to serve you." Joseph smiled, "As you wish, my friend." Timothy asked, "May I set the table?" Mr. Jones smiled, "Yes, that would be fine. Breakfast is almost ready."

As the men sat down to breakfast, they laughed and discussed the elaborate meal. Mr. Jones had fixed scrambled eggs, turkey bacon, hash browns, pancakes, and mixed fruit salad. Joseph asked, "Paul would you do the honor of saying grace?" Mr. Jones smiled, "I would love to." He bowed his head and closed his eyes, "Heavenly Father, Holy Spirit, and Jesus. We invite You to sit with us at our breakfast table. Lead us every day and thank You for my newfound friends. Thank You for Your presence. Amen."

The men started to serve themselves. Timothy was the first to speak, "Did you hear that?" He had stopped serving himself and was listening. Joseph and Mr. Jones listened. Timothy began to hum along to what he heard. Mr. Jones started laughing uncontrollably. Joseph smiled and shook his head, "Here it goes again." Mr. Jones asked amid his laughter, "Again?" Joseph smiled, "Yes! You are experiencing the

Joy of the Lord, which also happened on our flight." Joseph began to laugh.

Timothy was still humming. He said, "I believe I hear angels singing." Joseph listened between his laughter. Then he, too, heard the singing. Mr. Jones laughed so hard that he doubled over and fell onto the floor. He could not speak, just laughed. Then Timothy stopped humming. He listened, "I hear the Lord." Joseph and Mr. Jones were still laughing. Timothy listened, "I hear the Lord saying that I am supposed to decide if I want to work with you, Mr. Jones. He says it is my choice." Mr. Jones was still laughing but was getting back up and sitting on his chair. He looked at Timothy and said, "The offer is on the table until you decide. I am not going to pressure you. God has spoken."

As the men gather their composure, they discussed what they had just experienced. Mr. Jones was amazed, "I have never experienced laughter like this before. I had no idea that His presence can bring this much joy." Joseph and Timothy smiled at each other.

Joseph quietly spoke, "I am new to these supernatural experiences. When I feel His presence, I can sense a warm mantle or blanket covering me. I am learning not to be surprised by anything these days." Timothy added, "For me, it's only been a couple of days, and I can't wait to continue to learn more and experience more." Joseph smiled at his new friends.

The men attempted to finish their meal between talking and laughing. The taste of every bite they took was delicious. Finally, Joseph whispered, "I believe I can taste honey." Mr. Jones laughed as he answered, "I did not put any honey in this meal." Timothy added, "I taste apples too." Mr. Jones replied, "Nope, no apples added either!"

Mr. Jones remembered, "Psalm 19:10 They are more desirable than gold, yes than much fine gold, Sweeter also than honey and the drippings of the honeycomb. Psalm 17:8 Keep me [in Your affectionate care, protect me] as the apple of Your eye; Hide me in the protective shadow of Your wings."

Joseph smiled and said, "I want to be able to quote scripture like that someday." Mr. Jones added, "Psalm 37:4 Delight yourself in the LORD, And He will give you the desires *and* petitions of your heart." Joseph smiled and said, "I sure hope so." Mr. Jones responded, "I am not a Bible scholar, so this was the Lord speaking through me. I usually have a hard time memorizing scripture, but this was great that the Lord brought these verses to mind."

As the men finished breakfast, Joseph glanced at the time; it was just after 8:00. "Timothy, what time did you tell your sister we would arrive?" Timothy responded, "I told her between 9:30 and 10:00 but told her it might be closer to 10." Joseph knew they had to be on the road soon. He said, "Paul, Yah spoke to me out on the water, and I will arrange to come out to you after my vacation. I will not reach out to Samantha until a few days before the end because I have given her time off. I don't want her to work over her vacation." Mr. Jones replied, "I promise not to call her before she calls me. I know her value. I will leave my company's schedule open in two weeks for your first visit."

The men cleared the table and filled the dishwasher. Joseph smiled at the men, "I need to change out the clothes in my suitcase, so I better get to it. Paul, please feel free to stay as long as you like. I will leave my combination to lock the door on the counter. Timothy, I will be ready in a few minutes."

Timothy sat and visited with Mr. Jones after he grabbed his suitcase. Mr. Jones had already changed into his clothes and preparing to leave when the men left. Timothy and Mr. Jones exchanged numbers, and Timothy promised to contact him after the funeral services.

Joseph came out of his room with his suitcase and gym bag. The men hugged and said their goodbyes. Mr. Jones said, "Thank you again, Joseph. I knew it was important to meet with you but did not expect this blessing. We will talk in a couple of weeks and look forward to seeing you in Phoenix."

Chapter 11 Meet Timmie

The drive to Diamond Bar flew by quickly as the men spoke of family. Timothy wanted Joseph to know who he was about to meet. "MacKenzie is a huge sports fan. He loves the Lakers. He looks a lot like my dad. Jasmine is very feminine, soft-spoken, and is married to a lawyer. Karen, well, she is beautiful. Timmie, whom I have never met, will be a handful. I have only spoken to her a few times over the phone, and she appears to be super hyperactive. I am sure you will get along with them all, but I love Karen the best."

Joseph was smiling. "I am sure I will not have a problem with any of them. It's your family, and I know they will welcome me as your friend." Timothy suddenly asked, "I meant to ask why you brought a gym bag?" Joseph laughed, "Remember, I said I was a runner. If I cannot surf, then I run. Besides, I carry my towel everywhere I go."

They pulled up to the house at precisely 10:00. Timothy took a deep breath and silently prayed, 'I am ready to face whatever I need to. Lord, You are with me. Thank you for sending Joseph along.' Timothy said, "Well, here we go!"

Karen came running out of the house. She gave Timothy a big hug and began to cry. "I am so happy that you are here. I know mama knew you would come. Who do you have with you?" Timothy turned to introduce Joseph. "Karen, this is my friend Joseph. Joseph, this is Karen, my big sis whom I love." Joseph extended his hand to shake hands, but Karen leaned over and hugged him. She whispered, "Thank you for being Tim's friend. I can see how much he cares for you."

Joseph was a little confused, "Thanks. He is a good guy." Karen replied, "Yes, he is!" Just then, Timmie came running out of the house. "Uncle Timmie, Uncle Timmie! I am so happy you are finally here!"

She jumped into his arms. Timothy held her tight. Suddenly, he was overwhelmed; he did not expect to have feelings for a little girl he did not know. He whispered, "I am honored to meet you finally. I am so sorry it took so long." Timothy pulled her away so he could introduce her to Joseph, "Timmie, this is my friend Joseph."

Timmie turned and smiled, "Joseph. Joseph. Can I call you Joey?" Joseph smiled, "I don't know that anyone has ever called me Joey. Sure, that would be fine." Karen laughed, "Timmie, let's call him Joseph for now. Once you get to know him, maybe if it's okay with Joseph." Joseph smiled and winked at Timmie, "You may call me Joey. I like it!" Timmie threw her head back and gave an exaggerated laugh.

Karen asked, "Do you want to bring your luggage in right now?" Timothy answered, "Maybe later, Sis. Who's all here?" Karen replied, "It's just us for now. I did not let anyone know that you were coming in today. I thought it would be better to have you to ourselves." Timothy smiled, "Thanks! You're the best!"

Karen led the way, and Timothy was carrying Timmie. Joseph followed behind and admired this family connection. As they walked into the house, the aromas from the baked goods overtook them, and they began to laugh. Karen looked at the men, confused, and asked, "What's so funny." Timothy answered, "Oh, it's nothing, Karen; the aroma of the freshly baked cookies smells delicious." Karen was not sure what to make of the two men. Finally, Timmie said, "Mommy, it smells like heaven." Karen smiled, "I see."

Joseph explained, "Karen, we have been so sensitive to aromas in the last couple of days that it brings us to laughter. It's almost as if we have our sense of smell heightened." Karen was not sure what to say, "That's weird. Don't you think?" Timothy attempted to change the subject, "What did you bake?" Timmie responded before her mommy, "I baked you chocolate chip cookies! Mommy told me that you loved them when you were little like me." Timothy replied, "Oh, she did? Did she tell you that I could eat more than her?" Timmie laughed, "I can eat more than her too! You and I are the same, Uncle Timmie." Again, Timothy laughed, "Maybe we should have a contest to see who can eat the most?" Karen interjected, "NO! We are not going to do that today. We do not want to have a tummy ache, Timmie. Tomorrow is the day we celebrate grandma, remember?"

Timothy felt a little sad, "Sorry, I didn't think about the possible tummy ache. Timmie, we can do that another day. Is that okay?" Timmie smiled, "Yes, it's okay. Mommy, can we still eat some cookies?" Karen smiled at her daughter, "Yes, of course. You did bake them for your uncle." Timmie cheered, "Yay! Are you hungry now, Uncle Timmie?" Timothy looked at Joseph, "Are you hungry, Joseph?" Joseph laughed, "I am always hungry for sweets." Timmie cheered again, "Yay! Let's eat!" Karen apologetically added, "We have lots of fruit, veggies, and other baked goods. I can also make sandwiches if you would like. Do not feel forced to eat cookies unless you'd like." Joseph smiled at Karen, "Whatever you have is perfect. I eat every three hours, so I burn calories quickly. I don't worry about weight." Karen laughed, "I can tell you are in great shape. Me? I still have baby weight and hope to burn off one of these days." Joseph smiled, "You look wonderful. Don't let anyone tell you differently." Karen blushed, "Thank you. You are very kind to say that. Timmie, you have a good friend." Timothy responded, "Sis, you look marvelous! You are perfect and being a mom has been very good to you."

Karen was pulling out plates for everyone, "Please serve yourself whatever you'd like. We have plenty." Joseph was the first to speak, "Wow, Karen; this is a feast. Did you bake everything yourself?" Karen smiled bashfully, "I love to bake and cook. Mama was a great teacher. I have all her recipes and some of my own." Timothy added, "Sis, this is great. Thanks for everything. I mean everything." Karen knew what Timothy meant.

Timmie was busy telling her uncle and Joseph about the baking when she suddenly changed the subject. "My daddy died and went to heaven." Timothy was not sure what to say but attempted, "I know. I am sorry about your daddy." Timmie responded, "Oh, Uncle Timmie, don't be sorry. He is in Heaven. It is beautiful there. Someday I will go there too." Joseph asked, "Have you seen heaven, Timmie?" She lit up like a light, "I have gone to heaven." Joseph glanced at Karen, and she had tears running down her face. Joseph asked, "Karen, are you okay?" Karen nodded her head yes. Timmie continued, "I died, but I came back. Jesus said it was not my time. He told me to tell everyone about Heaven."

Timothy asked Karen, "Sis? Did Timmie die?" Karen shook her head yes. Timmie answered, "I did, Uncle. Mommy, how long ago was it?" Karen was struggling to speak, "Two months ago." Joseph reached over and gently placed his hand on Karen's. Timothy had tears running down his cheeks, "Sis, why didn't you call me?" Karen smiled, "There wasn't time. I called 911; we rushed to the hospital, and the next thing I knew, they told me she was gone. Mom and I fell to our knees and begged God not to take her. Then the nurses came out to get the doctor. She was back." Timothy replied, "I'm so sorry I wasn't here for you." Karen smiled, "You are here now. That's all that matters."

Timmie interrupted, "Heaven is so bright and beautiful, and the colors move. I got to see Jesus, and I played with Him. I asked Jesus where my daddy was, and He took me to see him. Daddy was not sick. Daddy hugged me and told me to come back and help mommy. Heaven is real. When we die, if we know Jesus, we go to live with Him. I saw grandpa too; he was very happy." Everyone was quietly listening. Joseph asked, "Did you eat in heaven?" Timmie laughed, "No, silly. I just played with Jesus." Joseph smiled, "That is nice. Thank you for sharing your story. You need to tell everyone so that they will believe and go to Heaven." Timmie responded, "That's what Jesus told me too."

Karen waited for a moment, then asked her brother, "Timmie, do you want the rest of the family to join us? I was selfish in wanting to keep you to myself." Timothy responded, "I am enjoying my time with you and Timmie. Maybe we can have them come tonight. I never did ask for the funeral details." Karen smiled, "I will call them later and invite them to dinner. The funeral service is on Monday. How long can you stay?"

Timothy answered, "I am not sure. I left an unfinished assignment in Europe, so I must return. The company told me to take my time, but I do not want to leave things too long. Let us see how the next couple of days go before I decide. How are Mac and Jazz?" Karen smiled, "They are doing well. They know mom is in a better place, and someday we will all be together again." Timothy asked, "So they believe in God?" Karen laughed, "I know what you must be thinking. They lived a hard life, but they are completely different people than the Mac and Jazz you knew. After Timmie shared her story, the whole family now believes. Timmie had never seen a picture of her great grandfather, but she described him to a tee after she came back to us."

Timothy was not sure what to believe. Joseph smiled and said, "Thank God for Timmie's experience. Timmie, you sure are going to lead people to Jesus." Karen added, "The whole church was in tears when they heard her tell her story. There have been many testimonies since Timmie shared her story." Timothy added, "I have experienced some pretty interesting things myself. Since I met Joseph, my life has also changed."

Karen's phone rang, "Hello Mac. What's up?"
"Yes, an old friend dropped by to say hello."
"Yes, our baby brother is here. I was selfish in keeping him to myself. Maybe you guys can come over for dinner?"
"Okay, that's fine. Go ahead and bring steaks for a BBQ."

Karen smiled at the men, "Well, guess who's coming to dinner?" Timothy responded, "It will be good to see everyone. It has been long enough." Karen asked, "Do you want to freshen up before dinner?" Joseph replied, "I'm good. We will get dirty at the BBQ, so why clean up?" Timothy laughed, "What do you think we will do?" Joseph asked, "I have always imagined the games played at BBQs."

Timothy explained, "He was an only child, so he hasn't been around family." Karen smiled, "Well, you will get to experience family tonight." Joseph asked, "Can we help prepare anything for tonight?" Karen replied, "Of course not! You are my guest, and MacKenzie likes to BBQ, so he will do all the work." Timothy asked, "When did he learn to BBQ?" Karen smiled, "After dad passed away, he took over all the BBQs." Timothy replied, "I see. I guess I wasn't around to see that."

Karen answered, "No, but you're here now. That is what matters. I love you, little brother." Timothy smiled, "Thanks, Sis."

Joseph had been observing the tenderness between the siblings. Timmie did not miss a beat, "I love you, Uncle Timmie. I love you too, Uncle Joey." Joseph smiled and said, "I love you, Timmie. I am so lucky to have met your uncle. He is the brother I never had." Karen hugged Joseph, "That makes you, my brother." Joseph chuckled. Timothy came over and joined in on the hug. Timmie jumped on Joseph, "That makes you, my uncle."

Chapter 12 Family Arrives

The doorbell rang, and Timmie ran to answer the door. She screamed with joy, "Uncle Mac! I am so happy to see you. Wait until you see Uncle Timmie. He looks just like me! He also brought my new Uncle Joey with him." MacKenzie laughed, "Thanks for filling me in on all the details, Timmie." Karen was laughing, "Nothing ever changes here." She gave her big brother MacKenzie a hug and asked, "Is it only you today?" MacKenzie answered, "Yeah, for now. Jessie and the girls will arrive around 7:30. They will be coming from dance. I know I'm a little early, but I wanted to get the grill ready."

As they headed out the back door, Timothy walked towards MacKenzie. He extended his hand, but MacKenzie pulled him in and gave him a bear hug. "How are you, little brother?" Timothy was surprised, "I'm doing well. How about you?" MacKenzie started to cry, "I sure missed you. I'm sorry I never reached out to you." Timothy was fighting back the tears, "it's okay. I didn't reach out either." Karen interrupted, "You are both here now. Nothing else matters." Timothy backed up and turned towards Joseph, "This is my friend Joseph." Timmie jumped in, "No! He's Uncle Joey." Joseph laughed, "That's right, and you better not forget that." Joseph opened his arms for that bear hug Timothy had just received. MacKenzie embraced Joseph, "Great to meet you, man."

Timmie was pulling at Joseph's shorts, "Come on, Uncle Joey. You were going to teach me to surf." She grabbed his hand and pulled him away. Joseph had prepared a board lying on the grass for the surf lesson.

MacKenzie asked, "Timothy, do you BBQ?" Timothy followed his older brother, "No, not really. Not home much." Karen followed the men.

MacKenzie replied, "You need to eat. Grilling is much easier than cooking inside." Karen laughed, "I don't know about that." Timothy smiled, "Well, I usually eat out, so I don't know much about cooking anything." Karen teased MacKenzie, "If all you eat is meat, maybe outdoor cooking is easier." MacKenzie laughed, "I cook veggies out here too." Karen pressed, "When?" MacKenzie added, "Starting today." Karen just laughed.

Timothy smiled and said, "I better go check on Timmie. Make sure she isn't drowning on the lawn." Karen followed her little brother, "He does love you. He isn't sure how you feel about him." Timothy answered, "I don't know what he expects after all these years. I don't know him." Karen replied, "So act like you just met him and make friends with him. Like when you met Joseph. How did you meet Joseph?" Timothy replied, "Maybe we can share that story when everyone is here, so we say that story once." Karen answered, "Okay, that sounds good. Joseph is doing well with Timmie. She seems to love him." Timothy said, "He is a great guy. I think everyone will love him. He is someone very different than most people I have met."

Timmie was laughing so loud that even MacKenzie turned to see what was happening. Joseph was giving instructions, "Ready, set, up." He would wiggle the board. Timmie was a quick study and had outstanding balance. Timothy grabbed a glass of water from the table. On Timmie's next jump up, he splashed her. She fell over in laughter. Karen scolded Timothy, "What are you doing?" Timmie screamed with joy, "The wave splashed me, mommy!" Everyone laughed.

Joseph spoke to Timmie, "I will have to take you with me so you can surf by my house." Timmie excitedly screamed, "Can I, mommy? Can I go with Uncle Joey?" Karen looked at Joseph, "She doesn't know how to swim yet, Joseph." Joseph did not skip a beat, "I will teach her. I am an excellent swimmer." Karen was unsure what to make of him, "I'm not sure the ocean is the first place to learn to swim." Joseph laughed, "Why not? She can learn anywhere. She is young and fearless. She's also a quick study." Timothy decided to rescue his sister, "What Karen is trying to say is that the ocean seems unsafe. Timmie is her only child." Joseph smiled, "If she can handle this water, the ocean isn't any different. She knows Jesus, and he will take care of her."

Timmie was tired of waiting for an answer, "Uncle Joey, when can we go surfing in the ocean?" Joseph smiled and looked at Karen, "When mommy says you can." Karen smiled and mouthed thank you to him. Timmie turned to Karen, "When can we go, mommy?" Karen looked at her precious daughter and knelt in front of her, "Timmie, first we must get through the services, the reception, and then we can decide when to visit your Uncle Joey. He works, so we must see when he will be home." Timmie smiled at Joseph, "Do you work tomorrow?" Karen knew she better save him, "Tomorrow is too early, Timmie. Can we talk about it later?" Timmie looked at Joseph, "You promise not to forget to invite me to surf?" Joseph smiled, "I promise. Let's take care of these things mommy needs to do first."

Suddenly there was a group of people walking into the backyard. MacKenzie hollered, "Steaks will be ready soon." Karen headed toward the group and greeted everyone. She started to make the proper introductions, "Everyone, this is Joseph. Please introduce yourselves." Timmie ran up and hugged everyone. She returned to Joseph and grabbed his hand, "Don't be shy, Uncle Joey. Clara, Kaila, Elijah, Logan, and Samuel are my cousins. They are all very nice." Joseph knelt and hugged each one. Suddenly, he fell over due to all the kids jumping on him. Joseph was laughing while trying to remove the kids off himself. The kids were all giggling and attempting to tickle him. Timothy headed over and started taking one kid off at a time. He greeted and hugged each one as he pulled them off. Timmie was the last one on Joseph.

Timothy laughed, "You have quite an effect on kids too." Joseph laughed, "I don't know what happened. Suddenly, I fell over." The kids were all still giggling. Timothy smiled, "Come on over; I'll introduce you to the adults." Joseph was still laughing as he greeted the adults. Timothy made the introductions, "Joseph, this is my sister Jasmine. Her husband, Hunter. McKenzie's wife, Jessie." Joseph hugged each one, "It's very nice to meet you."

Hunter asked, "What just happened with our kids?" Joseph replied, "I'm not sure. I think they had a plan to jump on me." MacKenzie replied, "My kids are normally very shy. I was pleasantly surprised." Joseph responded, "Timmie has been my buddy since I arrived." Hunter laughed, "Timmie doesn't know a stranger; she's so friendly, just like her mommy." Karen turned to address her brother-in-law, "What do you mean by that?" Hunter laughed, "I just mean she gets her bubbliness from you." Hunter asked, "So how do you know Tim?" Timothy laughed, "You won't believe this story."

Joseph began, "We were both traveling back to the States from Europe. I was sitting in my seat quietly resting when this guy sat beside me and started talking. I tried not to engage, but he persists. I finally gave in. I realized it is the Lord orchestrating this meeting. One thing led to another, and now we are like brothers. A brother I never had and always wished I did." All eyes were on Timothy. Joseph continued, "It was a very long flight, and we experienced some cool supernatural events." Karen asked, "How long have you known each other?" Timothy laughed, "Seems like an eternity, but I must be honest. It has only been a couple of days. I was excessively drinking coming home and quite stressed. I somehow sobered up immediately upon meeting Joseph. I felt like I had known him forever. I know it sounds weird, but it's true." Karen smiled, "I know I felt peace upon meeting Joseph. Timmie loves him, as you can tell. You know how careful I am with my girl."

Jessie glanced at MacKenzie, and he said, "I can tell you that I agree with Karen. I felt at peace with this young man. I observed him when I arrived, and I feel nothing but peace, love, and gentleness." Timothy added, "I didn't know what to expect, so I invited him. He was generous enough to reschedule his business meetings to help me out."

Joseph spoke, "I can assure you that I mean no harm to anyone. I am a consultant and do a lot of interventions with my clients. I heard the Lord tell me to come because there was much healing that needed to happen." Karen interjected, "Uncle Joey, please forgive us if we are making you feel unwelcome. After all, this is my house, and I have welcomed you with open arms. Anyone who is not comfortable is welcome to leave." MacKenzie added, "I believe my family is also very comfortable with you being here, Joseph."

Timmie could hear the conversation from her play area. She came running to Joseph and threw her arms around him. "Jesus told me that Uncle Joey is his friend. He said that he is going to help us." She then kissed Joseph on the cheek and said, "Thank you, Uncle Joey. We have all been very sad since grandma went to heaven." Joseph reached over to Karen and placed his hand on hers. "I heard the Lord say that you have had a heavy burden of caring for your elderly mother. All her pain is gone. She is watching from heaven to see her family come together to celebrate her life. The Lord says that you are not to worry. He is taking care of all the expenses. Someone will come to the door and give you a donation. It is a substantial donation, and all the funeral expenses will be paid in full. There will be plenty left over for you to do with as you see fit. The man will come today or tomorrow. He knew your mama. She was a great help to him when he needed a hand." Timmie smiled, "Yep, that's what I heard too."

Timothy looked at Karen, "Sis, are you struggling?" Karen had tears in her eyes, "Not really. We got by on my salary; however, mom was the one that took care of Timmie. Now I need to find someone to care for her until she can start school." Jessie spoke first, "Karen, I am sorry; I did not even think to ask if I could help. Please forgive me." Karen hugged her sister-in-law. "It would be great if she could come to you during the school year."

MacKenzie came over to Joseph, "How do you hear the Lord?" Joseph smiled, "I would be happy to explain and show you how to hear Him. Should we eat before the steaks get cold?" MacKenzie laughed, "Yes, let's all sit and eat. We can visit more as we eat." After everyone was seated, Karen asked, "Who would like to say grace?" Timmie shouted, "Let Uncle Joey!" Karen chuckled, "Joey, would you do the honor?" Joseph smiled shyly, "The honor would be mine." Timothy laughed, "Get ready, everyone." Joseph smiled and began, "Heavenly Abba, I thank you for this wonderful family. Thank you for bringing me here to enjoy this wonderful meal. Abba, Yeshua, and Ruach Haqodesh/Holy

Spirit, I invite you to join us as we break bread. Bless this home and family. I ask this in Yeshua/Jesus' name." Timmie chimed in, "Amen!" The family broke out in laughter. Timmie was sitting between Timothy and Joseph. She teased her Uncle MacKenzie, "I am sitting between my two favorite uncles." MacKenzie teased and pretended to be brokenhearted, "Oh, I am so sad. I am no longer your favorite. Boohoo!" Timmie laughed, "I am only teasing you, Uncle Mac. Don't cry. I love you too." MacKenzie smiled at her, "I love you too, Timmie."

As they enjoyed their meal, the children began to giggle uncontrollably. Timothy laughed, "The children are feeling the presence of the Lord. His joy." The adults watched the children in awe, not entirely understanding what was happening. They giggled as if they had just heard a good joke. Joseph started to laugh. He explained, "If you are feeling tingling or just feel like laughing. Surrender. That's the presence of the Joy of the Lord you feel." Timothy started to laugh. Karen began to giggle like a child. MacKenzie laughed at how silly things appeared. Then the others allowed the joy to flow. Timmie leaned on Timothy, and he fell over. Everyone laughed even harder.

Jasmine was finally able to speak, "How does this happen?" Joseph answered, "I am not sure, but every time I invite the Lord to join in, His presence overtakes us. We had many miracles on the flight home. It was quite supernatural." Jasmine said, "I have gone to church all my life, and nothing like this has ever happened. I feel overjoyed. I can cry without feeling sadness." The kids giggled even harder. Joseph replied, "I went to church with my mom, but when she passed away, I stopped going." Karen attempted to stop laughing but could not. Finally, she responded, "I am sorry to hear about your loss. How old were you?" Joseph laughed, "She's in heaven waiting for me; that's what matters." The laughter continued for quite some time.

Dinner was winding down when the presence lifted somewhat. Karen invited everyone to come inside, "Let's have dessert inside. It may be getting a little chilly for the children." Everyone grabbed their plates and headed inside. Timothy asked Timmie, "May I help?" Timmie laughed, "Yes, thank you, Uncle Timmie."

The living room was big and had comfortable couches. Everyone found a seat and continued to giggle. MacKenzie finally asked, "Joseph, tell me how you hear the Lord's voice." Joseph smiled, "Sure! Sometimes I hear Him audibly; other times, He is the quiet voice. Sometimes He is very loud in my ear or my mind. I also dream a lot. There are times that He has made me super sleepy, and as I rest, my head, I begin to dream. Occasionally, I see a vision while I am awake." Everyone was listening. Timmie laughed, "I see Jesus, and He tells me things." Kaila asked, "Timmie, what does Jesus look like?" Timmie smiled and began to speak, "Jesus is handsome and very tall. Taller than Uncle Mac! He wears white. Oh yeah, He is very bright." Kaila asked, "What do you mean, bright?" Timmie laughed, "He is shiny. He has lots of light. He has bright blue eyes, too. And He is very, very nice." Kaila laughed, "I wish I could see Jesus." Timmie laughed and pointed, "Look! He is right here!" Everyone looked; however, only the children could see Him.

Jasmine softly spoke, "We need to have childlike faith." Timothy smiled and said, "I felt like a child with all the laughter at dinner." Jasmine continued, "I think most of us tend to lose our imagination as adults. We need to have childlike faith so we can see and hear." Karen laughed, "I talk to the kids about using their imagination all day long. I never stopped to think that I may have lost it." Jessie added, "I cut hair all day long, and I must use my imagination when my customers ask me for something new. I have to imagine them with a new style. I think our imaginations have gotten too grown up. We only use it for work. Is there an exercise or something we can do to improve our imaginations?" Karen laughed, "That's a great idea, Jessie! I use visualization with students all the time. Maybe we can imagine Jesus, the way Timmie described Him."

She turned to face Timmie, "Can you stand by Jesus and describe Him?" Suddenly, all the children began to laugh. Timmie said, "He is teasing us. He is moving around the room. Jesus, would you please stand still so mommy can see you?" Kaila asked, "Auntie Karen, can you see Him. He is standing right in front of you." Karen frowned, "Not yet. What does He look like?" Samuel laughed, "He is wearing white pants and a white shirt." Elijah added, "His hair is dark brown." Timmie jumped in, "His eyes are very blue. And He has a big smile." Clara laughed, "Now He is standing in front of mommy." Timmie ran to her Auntie Jessie and started dancing. She said, "I am dancing with Jesus!" Suddenly everyone could see Him. They all jumped up and began to dance with Jesus. Timothy began to sing. He asked, "Do you hear the angels singing?" Karen stopped dancing and listened, "I hear them. The sound is Heavenly. Timothy, your voice is also Heavenly. I had almost forgotten how beautiful you sing."

Tears began to run down the children's faces. Hunter spoke, "Your singing is peaceful; it makes me feel warm and happy. Uncle Timmie, can you sing at grandma's service? I think the angels will sing with you." Timmie's eyes lit up, "Please, Uncle Timmie. You have to sing." Timothy had tears running down his face, "I don't know if I can sing in front of people. It has been so long." Jasmine looked at her younger brother, "Tim, I think mom would have loved to hear you sing again. She always bragged about your singing. She was so disappointed when you chose to go into business instead of music. I think she always imagined you as a rock star." Karen laughed, "I could picture you as a rock star. You would have long hair like Jesus. Wear tight pants and have an electric guitar." Laughing, MacKenzie added, "You might have to wear a headband to keep all that hair down." Finally, Timmie brought them all back to reality, "Uncle Timmie, you will sing because it makes Jesus very happy." Timothy smiled at Timmie. He knew he had to sing at his mom's funeral.

Jessie spoke, "I hate to break up this reunion; however, the kids have games in the morning. We need to get them to bed." Jasmine added, "The boys have a swim meet as well. We had better go too. Will you try to make it?" She was looking at Timothy. Timothy looked at Joseph and Karen, "Well, if we can. I am not sure what the plan will be for us." Karen rescued him, "It is very late, and these guys have been traveling. Let us see how early we wake up tomorrow. Timmie, say goodnight to everyone and go get ready for bed." Timmie attempted to delay her bedtime, "Mommy, I haven't finished playing with my uncles and Jesus." Karen answered, "They can come to tuck you in if you want. Say goodnight to everyone." As everyone prepared to leave, MacKenzie extended another invitation, "Hopefully, you won't be too exhausted from your traveling. Karen knows where we will be. If not, maybe we can have dinner again tomorrow. Joseph, it was a pleasure meeting you. I look forward to our next meeting. Timothy, glad you're home."

Chapter 13 Vibrating

Saturday was going to prove to be another exciting day. Joseph awoke with his body vibrating. He had never experienced this before. He asked, 'Why am I feeling this?' The bed felt like it was vibrating too. He thought to himself, 'No, it's just me.' He looked around, and he was alone in the bedroom. Although it was still dark out, he thought, 'Maybe I can get a short run before everyone awakens.' He got up, grabbed his gym bag, and pulled out his running shoes. As he got dressed for the run, he heard tiny footsteps.

Timmie knocked on his door. She whispered, "Uncle Joey? Can I come in?" Joseph walked to the door and opened it. "What's going on, Timmie?" She smiled at him, "I want pancakes. Can you make some?" Joseph chuckled, "Yes, I can. Do you want to eat now? It is early." Timmie had a grin from ear to ear, "Yes! Can you make mine smile?" Joseph laughed, "I can try. I have never done that, but I will try." Timmie took Joseph by the hand and led him into the kitchen. "Mommy usually makes the pancakes, and I get the syrup." Joseph laughed, "Okay, that sounds like a good plan. Can you show me where I can find everything?"

Timmie was a step ahead of everything that Joseph requested. "The flour and everything are here in the pantry. I can reach the syrup and chocolate chips." Joseph looked at Timmie, "Chocolate chips?" She laughed, "Yes, that's how you make the smile!" Joseph responded, "Oh, I see. Okay, that sounds good." As he grabbed the ingredients he needed, he heard some more footsteps.

Karen walked into the kitchen. "What are you two up to?" Timmie laughed, "We are going to make pancakes for breakfast." Karen stated, "Well, Joey is our guest, so we don't want him to cook for us." Timmie argued, "He will make me his special pancakes." Joseph laughed, "I am delighted to make the pancakes. It is my pleasure to serve this little Princess." Karen laughed, "Okay, but please allow me to do something." Joseph smiled, "What do you think, little Princess?" Timmie replied, "I think mommy should sit and watch. She can talk to us too." Karen threw her hands up, "Okay, but I will feel bored." Timmie laughed, "Mommy, it's not boring talking to us." Karen giggled, "That's not what I meant, Timmie. I am so used to making breakfast it feels funny not to be helping." Timmie added, "That's why we will fix breakfast for you, mommy." Joseph said, "Today, breakfast will be your special treat. It's about time someone treated you like a queen." Karen got teary-eyed, "It has been a long time." She looked at Timmie and smiled, "Daddy would be so proud of you."

Joseph asked, "Would you tell me about yourself and your family?" Karen smiled, "I would love to. Where should I start?" Joseph answered, "How about you start with how you met your husband and then go from there." Karen looked at Timmie and began, "Timmie, do you remember where I met daddy?" Timmie had a huge grin and answered, "At college!" Karen laughed, "Yes. I met Frank in my freshman year. He was leading a group of freshmen on a tour of the campus. He was a junior representative. We did not date until the following year. He finally got the nerve to ask me out on a date. He was the strong, quiet type. He was, is the love of my life." Karen's voice drifted off in thought. She continued, "He was a firefighter. There was a tragic fire." Karen's voice broke, "I'm sorry." There was a long pause. Joseph said, "I am sorry for your loss. You don't have to continue." Timmie jumped in, "Mommy tell Uncle Joey about when I was born." Karen wiped her tears away, "Well, that was the best day of my life. Timmie came into the world much too early. She was kicking and fighting to come out. She wanted to meet her mommy and daddy." Karen laughed, "When she was born, she only weighed four pounds. She surprised us because we didn't expect her to arrive for another month." Timmie added, "Yeah, I was crying when I came out. Daddy said he could hear me when I was still inside mommy's belly."

Joseph laughed, "Wow! That is an amazing story! You must have strong lungs. And a loud voice for you to do that!" Timmie was giggling. Karen laughed, "She was such a busy girl from the time she was born. We could not believe how much Timmie talked. She was very vocal from the very start. When Timmie was hungry, she let us know. When she was wet, Timmie let us know. She has been such a beautiful blessing. I love you, baby girl!" Timmie laughed, "I know you do, mommy! I love you more!" Karen laughed and explained, "Daddy always said that. It did not matter who told him that they loved him. He always would say he loved them more."

Joseph laughed, "Sounds like you had a pretty awesome daddy." Timmie laughed, "He was the best! He always played with me. Daddy built that treehouse for me before I was even born. He built me a dollhouse before I was born. He even picked my name!" Joseph asked, "He did all those things for you? That's so awesome!" Timmie added, "He knew that my mommy loved her little brother, so he said that my name should be the same. So, she can always think of him when she calls my name." Karen was smiling, "It was a rough time, but Frank was so supportive."

Joseph asked, "Timmie, can you check on your uncle to see if he is joining us for breakfast?" Timmie jumped off her chair and ran screaming, "Uncle Timmie! Uncle Timmie! Breakfast is ready. Are you coming to eat?" Timothy came around the corner about the same time. "I am ready. What did you make for breakfast that smells so yummy?" Timmie answered, "We made pancakes!" Joseph was placing all the food on the table. Joseph exclaimed, "Soups on!" Timmie laughed, "I haven't heard that in a long time. That's what daddy used to say."

Joseph glanced over at Karen, "I'm sorry. I am not sure why I said that. I don't normally." Karen smiled, "it's okay. Occasionally, I believe God has someone say that to let me know He is watching over me." As they sat down, Joseph asked, "Timmie would you like to say grace?" Timmie smiled, "Yes, I will!" She bowed her head, "Dear Jesus, thank you for sending both of my uncles. Bless Mommy, Uncle Timmie, Uncle Joey, and me. Thank you for taking daddy to heaven with you. Amen."

Timmie laughed when Joseph placed her plate in front of her. Joseph asked, "What's so funny?" Timmie said, "Look. It looks like my pancake is an angel. See the wings?" Joseph laughed, "I had not noticed. I guess they are extra special for you." Timmie looked at every pancake, "Only mine have wings!" Karen laughed, "I guess God sent you special pancakes today." Timmie giggled, "Yes, He did!"

They were enjoying breakfast and conversation when they heard a knock on the door. Karen went to answer. Timothy followed her.

As she opened the door, an older gentleman smiled, "Hello. I am not sure if you know me." Karen and Timothy shook their heads no. He continued, "I am Abraham Gonzalez. I heard your mom had passed away. May I come in?" Karen spoke first, "Yes, of course. Please excuse my silence. I do not understand why you are here. Or how you knew my mom." Timothy added, "We are having breakfast. Would you like to join us?" Joseph was ahead of the game. He was setting an extra place at the table. Timmie asked Joseph, "How did you know?" Joseph smiled and teased, "You know how." Timmie giggled, "Jesus told you! He told me too."

As the threesome entered the dining room, Timmie greeted Mr. Gonzalez, "Hello, Mr. Gonzalez. We have been waiting for you." He smiled and asked, "You have?" Timmie laughed, "Yes, Jesus told Uncle Joey and me that you were coming today for breakfast." Mr. Gonzalez chuckled loudly, "He did?" Timmie continued, "Yes. We made extra pancakes for you."

Karen asked, "How did you know our mom?" As Mr. Gonzalez served himself, he answered, "I met your mom at a homeless shelter. I was down on my luck. Maybe instead of saying luck, I should say that I was disobedient. Anyway, your mom brought food to serve that day. She looked radiant. I had never seen anyone look like that before. I asked her why she looked radiant. She laughed and said, 'it was Jesus I saw.' I told her I did not believe in this Jesus guy. She told me that Jesus told her she would meet me. She even knew my name. That made me listen. She told me that Jesus had been after me for years. I kept saying no. She said, 'Today is the day you have to choose." Timothy asked, "You said she knew your name? How did she know your name? Your full name?" Mr. Gonzalez laughed, "That's how I reacted when she said, 'Your name is Abraham Gonzalez. You lost your family in a fire, that you had accidentally started while sleeping on the couch. Smoking is a bad habit, and today you will stop smoking."

He paused, then continued, "Yep, that's the look I had on my face." He was smiling at Karen and Timothy. Timmie was silently listening about her grandmother. Joseph quietly spoke, "Words of knowledge. Nice!" Mr. Gonzalez continued, "I said to her, 'I have smoked for fifty years, and I am not going to quit just because you said to.' She laughed and said, 'I am not the one telling you. God is.' So just for spite, I lit a cigarette. Do you know that it would not light? Finally, I got it to light, and when I tasted it, the flavor was so bad I felt I would throw up."

Timothy was in shock. "I never knew my mom was like that." Karen echoed, "I didn't either." Timmie laughed, "I did!" Everyone laughed. Mr. Gonzalez continued, "So she asked, 'what's your decision?' I asked, 'about what?' She laughed, 'you must decide. Do you want to change your life?' I nodded yes, and she said, 'here is the first $100 to help you change your life.' She walked away from me. I followed her and asked, 'why would you give me $100?' She said, 'because Jesus told me to.' I thought, 'wow if Jesus does exist, He must love me.' She turned around and said, 'yes, He does love you.' She would come to the shelter and teach about Jesus for the next few years, and then suddenly she stopped coming." Karen spoke up, "That must have been when she got sick." Mr. Gonzalez answered, "It must have been. I got my act together with the Lord's help, and I now own multiple businesses. I thank God for your mom every day. For her obedience."

Timothy looked at Joseph, "I know what you're thinking. Mom's prayers helped to send you to me. Right?" Joseph laughed, "You said it." Karen added, "Mom always prayed for her baby. She loved you so much." Karen looked at Mr. Gonzalez, "Thank you for sharing this story about mom. We had no idea. She never spoke of this. It was something that she kept quiet. Thank you, Mr. Gonzalez." Mr. Gonzalez added, "That's not all."

He smiled and opened his wallet. "I heard the Lord say that I needed to help you. I want to take care of all the funeral expenses. I have this for you." He handed Karen a check.

Karen looked at the check in shock. "Mr. Gonzalez, I don't know how to say thank you. This check is very gracious. It is more than I need for the funeral." Mr. Gonzalez answered, "You can do whatever you see fit with the remainder." Karen was staring at the $50,000 check. "I can't believe this." She stammered. Mr. Gonzalez smiled and said, "This isn't even enough to say thank you to your mom. I know when she gave me the $100, she was giving all she had. It is like the widow's mite in the Book of Mark in the Holy Scriptures. She taught me to be obedient. I will never forget her. Please do not hesitate to reach out to me." He handed Karen his business card. He then said, "I must get going. Thank you so much for your hospitality. I will be unable to attend the funeral services but will be there in spirit. I leave today for a meeting in South America."

The family walked Mr. Gonzalez out to the front door. They said their goodbyes and promised to keep in touch.

The family was still in shock. They did not know as much as they thought they knew about their mom; after meeting Mr. Gonzalez, they had an idea for the service. They decided that they should celebrate her life by asking everyone in attendance to share a story. Timothy added, "We should record it, so the future generations will know how special their grandmother was." Karen agreed, "I think that is a great idea. I bet we will learn more about mom. The Lord used her, and we had no idea." Timmie was laughing. "I want to know more about grandma, too, mommy."

Karen changed the subject, "I got a text from MacKenzie asking if we would come over for a BBQ at 1:00. How does that sound for you?" Timothy replied, "I'm good if everyone else is." Joseph nodded his head yes, "I am here as your guest, so I am open to anything Yah has for us." Timothy laughed, "Will you ever say no?" Joseph chuckled,

97

"Yeah, I will when I hear a no." He added, "Well, I thought I would get a run in this morning; however, Timmie had other plans. If you don't mind, I will run up and shower." Timmie shouted, "You better hurry, Uncle Joey, because I want to play outside." Joseph laughed and said, "Okay, maybe I will shower later. I am going to sweat outside." He motioned for Timothy to come out too. Joseph headed out, led by his hand by Timmie, who was happily skipping as she led Joseph. Timothy headed out behind them.

Karen followed, too; however, she was in deep thought about what had just happened with Mr. Gonzalez. She realized that her mom was even more impressive than she had believed. Karen wondered, 'How many people did she impact? What lives did she affect, and yet I knew nothing? She was so humble and loving.' Karen sat and watched Joseph. He was back to teaching Timmie how to surf. She was doing very well, considering she was only four years old. She watched as her daughter jumped up onto the board. She wondered, 'Does Timmie have the same or similar gifts as mom?' Karen was startled to hear the voice say, 'Yes.' Karen turned and looked around. Timothy was too far away to have answered Karen. Joseph was busy with Timmie. She asked again, 'Does Timmie have the same or similar gifts as mom?' 'Yes.' She heard that voice again. She whispered, "Lord, is that you?" 'Yes.' Karen stood up and turned around. She looked around but saw nothing.

Timmie looked over at her mom and yelled, "He is right beside you, mommy." Karen turned to face Timmie, "Who is?" Timmie laughed, "Jesus!" Karen sat down and smiled. Timothy had turned and was watching his sister. Joseph smiled, "Mommy is not sure she hears His Voice." Timmie laughed, "It is real, mommy!" Karen sat feeling shocked, "I thought I imagined things." Timothy came over and put his arm around her. "It's okay, Sis. Just know that He is always with you." Joseph had walked over too, "He is as close as your breath. From this day forward, expect to experience His presence." Timmie had joined the adults and climbed up on her mommy's lap.

Timmie laughed, "Mommy, didn't grandma ever tell you stories of her talks with Jesus?" Karen shook her head no. "Well, she used to tell

me, and she always talked with God. Every day she talked to Him."
Karen stated, "She always said she spoke to God, but I thought she just
imagined it. I didn't realize she spoke to Him and heard Him." Timothy
laughed, "Me either." Joseph said, "It all happens in His timing. It is
your time now." Karen smiled, "You're right. I only wish I had known
more about mom. I knew she was close to the Lord. I guess I was just
too busy to take the time to talk to her about this." Timothy hugged
his sister, "You were here for her. She was here for you too. Timmie
got to know her and learn from her. You know that is what is
important. You did the best you could in your situation. You were
here, and she knew it."

Timmie giggled, "Grandma always spoke to God. Jesus would make her
giggle. One day, she asked if I could hear Him too, and I did." Karen
smiled at Timmie, "I didn't know that." Timmie was giggling, "I know. I
didn't tell you because you didn't ask."

Timothy laughed, "I guess we need to ask more questions. Timmie, did
grandma see Jesus?" Timmie was laughing, "No, she did not. She saw
God."

Joseph looked at his watch, "I better shower. Time sure flies when
you're having fun."

As they loaded up in Karen's van, Timothy asked Karen, "Do you realize
that Joseph gave the word about Mr. Gonzalez?" Karen answered,
"Yes. I was thinking about that." Timothy asked, "Joseph, how do I get
filled more with the Lord?" Joseph chuckled, "Thought you'd never
ask!" Karen asked, "I want more of the Lord too."

Joseph said, "All you need to do is ask Ruach Haqodesh, aka Holy Spirit,
for more. Ask Him to come in and manifest His presence in your life.
Have you received the Holy Spirit baptism?" Timothy replied, "No,
what's that?" Karen asked, "Is that different than a water baptism?"

Joseph replied, "Yes, it is. I paraphrase, of course, but Mark 16 says
that if we believe and are water baptized, we will be saved from Yah's
or God's wrath and judgment; those that do not are condemned. In
Mark 1:8, John the Baptist says that His baptism (referring to Jesus,

Yahushuah HaMashiach), a holy baptism by the Ruach Haqodesh, will change you from the inside out. In Acts 2, the apostles say to receive the Holy Spirit, the Ruach Haqodesh. Yahushuah HaMashiach says in the Book of Luke to his disciples not to leave Jerusalem until they receive the Ruach Haqodesh or Holy Spirit. So, all that to say, it is important to receive baptism by the Ruach Haqodesh and water."

Timmie was the first to respond, "I want to!" Timothy smiled at her, "Maybe you're too young." Joseph laughed, "If she understands what she's asking for, then she's not. You are never too young to be filled with the Spirit." Karen added, "I would like too as well. I want all the Lord has for me." Timothy asked, "When can we do this?" Joseph laughed, "Maybe we should wait until you're not driving, Karen." Karen laughed, "Okay, when we arrive at Mac's." Joseph laughed, "Sure! Let's see who else wants more." Timmie responded, "Everybody wants more of God. Don't they?" Karen stated, "We can ask!"

Chapter 14 I See Jesus

As they entered Mac's home, Timmie started to giggle. "I can already see that Jesus is here." Timothy and Joseph smiled at each other. Karen responded, "Jesus is everywhere; He is in our hearts. Therefore He is everywhere with us. He goes before us to every place we go."

MacKenzie had heard them arrive and was coming in from the backyard to greet them. "Everyone is in the pool. I hope you all brought your swim trunks?" Karen apologized, "I'm sorry, I forgot to mention that to the guys. Please forgive me?" Timothy was the first to respond, "Well, I am in shorts, so that should suffice." Joseph laughed, "Yep, me too." Timmie added, "I always have my swimsuit here, so I never have to bring some." Karen said, "I guess I am the only one not swimming today." MacKenzie laughed, "Good try, sis. You can use one of the swim trunks here. We have extra towels out by the pool. The last one in is a rotten egg." And with that, they all raced to the pool.

They were having a great time in the pool and had lost track of time. Suddenly the kids start to complain of hunger. MacKenzie got out and headed to the kitchen for the steaks. Timothy and Joseph also got out and offered to help. MacKenzie smiled, "Well, if one of you wants to start the grill. I could use some help bringing out the steaks and hot dogs." Timothy headed to the grill. Joseph helped MacKenzie.

Joseph asked, "MacKenzie, what's your story?" MacKenzie smiled, "What do you mean?" Joseph added, "Well, tell me anything you would like. Your life, your job, whatever you want. Or shall I say whatever God wants you to?"

MacKenzie thought, "Well, I am the oldest of the bunch. I always felt I had to be the tough one and set an example for the younger ones. I loved my mom and dad. I especially had a great relationship with my dad. When he passed away, it was very hard on me. We all had it rough, but he was my best friend. I lost the person I could talk to about anything and everything. I did not know what to do, so I kept quiet and held it all in. Years later, when I met my wife, she filled that void." He glanced over at Joseph, who listened quietly and then continued, "She helped me realize that my dad had shown me how to love. I had a new understanding of mom. I realized that she was truly dad's best friend. I then saw how much she missed him. I never really knew how to talk to the girls or Timothy. He was always that baby brother that mom spoiled. When she lost both, I truly saw her pain. You would have thought I would have called Tim, but I could not. It was too painful. Every time I thought about it, it brought dad's death to the forefront. Then after a few years had gone by, I was afraid that he wouldn't speak to me. I thought he would blame me."

Joseph asked, "How do you feel now?" MacKenzie answered, "I still feel guilty for not reaching out." Then, Joseph asked, "Would you like to get rid of the guilt?" MacKenzie smiled, "Absolutely! Is it possible?" Joseph answered, "Yeah, it is. After dinner, maybe all the siblings can sit to pray and talk." MacKenzie smiled, "That would be great!"

Dinner was delicious and filled with laughter. After dinner, the kids all went upstairs to play. Then, the adults grabbed a glass of water and sat in the living room.

Joseph began, "I would like to open in prayer before speaking. Is that alright?" Everyone answered, "Yes, of course." Joseph continued, "Yah, you are always with us. You are the God of Abraham, Isaac, and Jacob. We invite you to join us here for this family prayer time. For this time of healing. Thank you, Yah, for what you are getting ready to do with this family." Joseph paused, then continued, "These past few years, this family has suffered much pain. I would say that some suffered alone while Karen, you, were able to lean on your mom. Am I right?" They all shook their heads in agreement. Joseph smiled, "Forgiveness is something that you need to speak out loud. The adversary needs to know that you are serious. Can you ask the others for forgiveness for not being available for each other and then forgive yourselves? Just speak what's in your hearts."

Timothy went first, "Karen, Jasmine, and Mac. Please forgive me for running away. For not being here for you. For staying away for so long. I am so sorry I was not here for mom. I was afraid to come home. I was angry because I wanted to have a better relationship with dad, and I knew that was no longer an option. I could not stand to see mom in pain; therefore, it was easier to stay away. Once I stayed away, it was hard to come back. I envied you, Mac, for your relationship with dad. I blamed you because I felt he did not love me as much as he loved you. Karen, forgive me for leaving you alone when you needed me most. Jasmine, forgive me for not being a better brother to you. Jasmine, I am sorry; please find it in your heart to forgive me." Everyone was in tears. Joseph encouraged them, "Say I forgive you, Timothy." They all spoke the words of forgiveness.

MacKenzie asked, "May I go next?" They all nodded yes and wiped tears away. MacKenzie gathered himself and knelt before Jasmine, "Jasmine, forgive me for not being there for you. For ignoring your calls. For avoiding meeting with you. For texting instead of calling you. For not being the big brother, I should have been. Please forgive me, sis." Jasmine cried uncontrollably and threw her arms around MacKenzie, "I have forgiven you. I love you, Mac."

MacKenzie then knelt before Karen, "Karen, my beautiful baby sister. Forgive me for blowing you off when you called for help. Forgive me for telling you that you were too emotional and that I could not handle you. Forgive me for being so distant. Forgive me for not being there when you lost Frank. It brought dad's death back, so I avoided you like the plague. Karen, I am sorry; please forgive me, baby sister." Karen hugged her big brother, "I have forgiven you. I love you, Mac. Thank you for being so good to Timmie. I love you."

MacKenzie then went to Timothy and knelt before him. "Tim, forgive me for hogging dad. I never thought about how you must feel. Forgive me for not reaching out to you, and please forgive me for always picking on you. Forgive me if I made you feel less than. Forgive me for abandoning you when dad went to heaven. I did not know what to say to you. I was angry that you did not make time for us. Please forgive me." Timothy hugged his brother. "All is forgiven. I love you, Mac."

Jasmine spoke next, "Mac forgive me for being so angry with you. For not understanding how much pain you felt. Forgive me for not being here when you needed help, Karen. Forgive me for thinking that you had it all under control and did not need the help for not appreciating all you did for mom. Tim, forgive me for not trying to be a good big sister to you. For not reaching out to you. For thinking that you were acting like a spoiled brat. Forgive me for not being the sister each one of you deserved." They all got up and hugged her. They spoke the words of forgiveness to her.

It was Karen's turn. Karen smiled at each of her siblings and softly spoke, "Forgive me for feeling like giving up on all of you. God kept telling me not to give up. I felt like a nag. I was always calling each of you, trying to get you to engage. I cried each time you did not answer, but I forgave you because I knew you were all hurting. Forgive me for not knowing what to do for each of you. Mom always told me that I needed to forgive you, so I did. Mom loved each of you so much. I love each of you so much." MacKenzie spoke first, "Karen, I forgive you, but there is nothing to forgive. You acted like the older sibling. You're awesome!" Timothy agreed, "You never gave up on us, sis. I love you!" Jasmine added, "You are the best sister! Also, the most patient. Thank you."

Joseph waited and then added, "Now, I would like you to forgive yourselves. Give it all up to Yah. Give Him the guilt, the shame, whatever you have been holding on to."

They all spoke self-forgiveness at the same time. Joseph asked, "Who wants to receive the Holy Spirit Baptism?" They all jumped up, raised their hands, and shouted I do. Joseph smiled and said, "Okay then. Just say, Lord, fill me with Your Holy Spirit." He walked to each one and lightly placed his hand upon their heads. The moment that he touched each one, they fell under the Power of the Holy Spirit.

The children heard all the commotion and came running downstairs. Timmie laughed, "I want Holy Spirit too!" Joseph laughed and touched her head. She fell and started giggling. The other children lined up, and each fell giggling. Joseph began to sing Joshua Aaron's 'You are Holy.' As he praised and worshipped, the others joined in after their experiences.

After they had worshipped for some time, they began to share their experiences. To their surprise, they each had a different experience. Finally, Karen started to share what she had experienced. "I can see angels in the room. They are huge. They were each waiting for an assignment. They received a scroll when we spoke in our spiritual language and flew away. There were many angels, and they were busy coming and going. It was amazing."

Timothy began to describe what he saw. "I saw the angels that worship God. They said, 'Holy, Holy, Holy is the Lord God Almighty. Who was, who is, and is to come.' I saw the creatures or angels that were around the throne. They had six wings and eyes everywhere. There are four of them. I saw four faces on each, a lion, an ox, a man, and an eagle. Every time the creatures gave glory to God. I saw the twenty-four elders who all had thrones around God. They would fall before God and worship Him. I couldn't believe what I was seeing." Joseph said, "Wow! You saw what the Book of Revelation speaks of in chapter 4." Karen confirmed, "Yes, it is chapter 4."

The kids were still giggling on the floor. Jasmine described her experience. "I didn't see anything. I felt as if someone was rubbing my hands, almost like caressing the backs of my hands, so gentle. I opened my eyes, wondering who it was. There was no one, so I closed my eyes and continued to experience the rubbing. It felt so cool and refreshing. I did not want to get up because of the peace and joy. It was wonderful."

MacKenzie laughed, "I had a vision of the dry bones that Ezekiel saw. I saw a valley full of human skeletons. Then I heard God say prophesy to these dry bones. I spoke the words he told me. Then I saw the tendons, ligaments, muscles, organs, and skin grow back onto the skeletons. Then God said, 'Prophesy to the breath, to the four winds so that these men will live again. Therefore, I did as He commanded me to. I saw the wind blow, and breath entered their nostrils. They got up, and they were a mighty army. I had never experienced anything like that."

Jessie asked, "Mac, you saw all of that?" MacKenzie smiled, "Yes, honey, I did. What did you experience?" Jessie hesitated, then spoke, "I saw myself at a ball. I had a beautiful blue lace gown. It was a long and flowing gown. I had a crown on my head. I then saw Jesus come up to me and take my hand. We began to dance. Everyone on the floor moved back and watched us dance. He made me feel like a princess." She looked at Mac, "I couldn't believe how happy I felt. It was like I was dancing with you because he knew every movement I made." Mac smiled at his wife, "It's okay, honey. I understand; Jesus danced with you. You don't have to feel bad about it."

Jessie replied, "I felt so happy, and I feel guilty that someone else made me feel happier than I feel on earth." Joseph interrupted, "Jessie, we are supposed to feel happier than anything we can imagine when we spend time with Jesus." Tears were rolling down Jessie's face, "Does this mean that I am not happy with you, Mac?" MacKenzie hugged his wife, "No, honey, it doesn't mean that. You should be so happy and in love with Jesus that nothing else matters. Do not feel bad. Enjoy how you felt. Enjoy your vision. You needed to experience this." Joseph added, "Sometimes, we feel that something is missing in the natural. Jesus fulfills every need we have." Jessie sobbed, "I feel so happy that I can't stop crying. I want to feel like this every day."

Elijah sat up and asked, "Mommy, are you okay?" Jessie laughed, "Yes, sweetie. I am wonderful." He asked, "Why are you crying, mommy?" Jessie laughed even harder, "Jesus makes me so happy that tears keep coming down my face." Elijah began to laugh too.

Elijah asked, "Daddy, can I tell you what I saw?" MacKenzie answered, "Yes, please." He was still laughing, "I saw heaven. I saw all kinds of animals. There were lions and deer, lambs, cats, and dogs. They were all playing together. No one was hurting or trying to eat anyone. Then I saw a baby. Jesus told me that the baby was my little brother. He looked just like me but did not have a name. He was waiting for his name. Can I give him a name?" Jessie and MacKenzie looked at each other, quite surprised. Finally, MacKenzie spoke, "Elijah, you were a twin. We lost your little brother before you came out of mommy's tummy." Jessie whispered, "Elijah, what do you want your twin brother's name to be?" He smiled, "I heard Nathan when I was in heaven. However, the spelling was different. N A T A N." Mac replied, "That is a perfect name. Thank you."

Timmie was next to speak, "I was playing in a meadow with Jesus and all the puppies. They were all singing to Jesus and me. They licked my face too. That's why I was giggling."

Samuel was still giggling. He spoke up between his giggles. "I was running so fast that I started flying through the sky. I was flying so fast that all I could hear was the air. There was singing in the air; it was as if the notes were floating all around me. Every time I ran into one of the notes, it tickled me. It was as if they were real. With everyone singing, the notes just kept floating up to me. The notes were almost like balloons. Each one made a different sound. I just kept running into them."

Kaila was smiling, "I got to see all the sea animals. I could breathe underwater. I saw animals that I had never seen before. Some were big, and some were very small. I saw very colorful underwater animals. They spoke to me; it was as if we spoke without using our mouths. I knew what they were saying and understood them. Then I came out of the water and saw land animals and flowers. The flowers seemed to be alive. It was as if the colors moved. It was amazing and beautiful."

Joseph smiled, "Do you see how unique each experience is? God has created each of us with unique dreams and visions. He thought of us before the world was created. He thought much about how we would see the world and heaven. He truly loves each one of us."

Karen spoke after a moment of silence. "I hate to break up our fun, but it is very late. We have church in the morning. I am teaching Sunday school. So, I better get some sleep."

They said their goodbyes and headed home.

Sunday morning, Joseph awoke early and went for his run. As he ran, he heard Yah saying, 'Job well done, son! Your assignment is complete. This family has received healing, and you have activated them. Enjoy your time!' Joseph smiled as he thought about the experiences everyone had experienced. He was happy that Yah was pleased with him. He thought, "Use me as you wish, Papa. Increase my discernment. I am ready for whatever you have for me. Thank you, Papa, for choosing me to meet this beautiful family." Joseph had been gone for an hour and was on his way back when he thought about his meeting coming up with Ahanu Fowler. He wondered, 'What if he is my relative? How will we feel when we discuss our lives?' Joseph heard Yah say, 'I have already written everything about you. Do not worry or stress about anything. You are My son, My creation. Everything else is a minor detail of your life. I am eternal.' Joseph spoke aloud, "Yes, Yah! I hear you. I am grateful for all You do in my life. I love You, Papa!" Then Joseph heard, 'This family is part of your new family.'

Timmie was waiting for Joseph. He could smell that someone had been busy making breakfast. Timmie greeted Joseph, "Good morning, Uncle Joey! I have been waiting for you." Joseph laughed, "You have? You were a sleepy head this morning." Timmie made a funny face, "I was not! I woke up, but you were already running out the door. So, you did not hear me call you." Joseph replied, "I am sorry; I must have been in deep thought." Timmie laughed, "it's okay. I woke up Uncle Timmie, and he made us breakfast. I think mommy is still sleeping, so I will give her breakfast in bed." Joseph chuckled, "That is a great idea. She is going to love it." Timmie laughed, "She hasn't had breakfast in bed since daddy, and I made her some." Joseph replied, "Then she will probably be amazed." Timmie giggled, "I hope so. I went and peeked in on her, but she was still sleeping. Can we all go into her room?"

Joseph smiled, "I don't think your mommy would want Uncle Timmie and me to see her in her PJs and sleepy." Timmie answered, "She wouldn't care. I want us all to surprise her." Joseph answered, "Well, maybe Uncle Timmie can. I need to shower because I am stinky." Timmie laughed, "No, you're not. I don't smell anything." She breathed in, "All I smell is sausage and biscuits." Timmie giggled. Joseph smiled, "Well, let's see what your uncle says. Is everything ready?" Timmie took Joseph by his hand, "Yes. We need to sneak in on my mommy."

Joseph looked at Timothy as he entered the kitchen. "So, what's the plan?" Timothy laughed, "Well, you arrived just in time to eat. Timmie is going to surprise her mommy." Timmie interrupted, "Excuse me, Uncle. We are going to surprise mommy." Timothy laughed, "Well, I think mommy would like to enjoy breakfast in bed with her princess. Not two strange guys." Timmie laughed, "You are not strange." Timothy made a funny face at his niece, "I'm not?" She laughed, "Okay, maybe you are."

Karen walked into the kitchen, "What is everyone doing up so early?" Timmie turned to face her mom, "What are you doing up, mommy? I was going to bring you breakfast in bed." Karen replied, "Oh my. I should have stayed in bed. Well, I am up now to join you all here." Timmie made a pouty face, "That's not fair. I wanted to surprise you." Karen smiled and hugged her little girl, "I am so sorry I ruined your surprise. I could smell the delicious aromas from the kitchen, and I woke up." Timmie continued, "But I wanted to surprise you." Karen laughed, "I am surprised. My bed is not big enough for all of us to climb into bed. I don't want Uncle Timmie and Joey to feel sad because they don't fit." Timmie replied, "Okay, mommy. I guess we can eat here."

They laughed and enjoyed breakfast. As the family finished, they discussed the funeral plans. The day would go uneventful and fly by quickly. On Monday, after the funeral service and reception, Joseph knew it was time to head back to Manhattan Beach.

He sat down and spoke to Timmie, "I need to go home. I have a friend coming to stay with me for a week. You can come to visit anytime you like, and I will give you surf lessons." Timmie began to cry, "I don't want you to go, Uncle Joey. I want you and Uncle Timmie to stay here with mommy and me forever." Joseph felt sad, "I am so sorry, honey, but I can't do that; I must work. Maybe when mommy gets out of school for the summer, you can come to visit. You can also come to see me any weekend." Timmie looked up at him, "How many days is that?" Joseph was not sure how to respond, "I'm not sure. The two of you can discuss that, and you are always welcome. Even if I am not home, my home is always open to you. Sometimes I work a lot."

Psalm 90:2

Before the mountains were born
Or before You had given birth to the earth
and the world,

Even from everlasting to everlasting,
You are the Eternal God.

Chapter 15 Ahanu

Joseph was headed west on Highway 60 to Los Angeles International Airport. He was excited to meet with his friend Ahanu Fowler. He was his possible look-alike relative. Suddenly his phone rang on his Bluetooth, "Ahanu, how was your flight?" Ahanu answered, "It was shorter than I expected." Joseph laughed, "It's quite alright. I should be there in 20 minutes." Ahanu answered, "Take your time. I will pick up my luggage and wait in front of Frontier Airlines." Joseph joked, "What do you look like? I want to make sure I don't miss you!" The men laughed. Joseph added, "See you soon! I will give you a call as I arrive at the airport."

Joseph dialed Ahanu. Ahanu answered, "Hello, Joseph." Joseph laughed, "How did you know it was me?" Ahanu answered, "Purely luck, I believe." Joseph replied, "I guess I better be on my best behavior then." Ahanu answered, "No need, buddy. What are you driving?" Joseph chuckled, "Remember I mentioned I had an older car?" Ahanu laughed, "Am I supposed to be looking for a clunker?" Joseph replied, "Well, kind of, I guess. I'm in a green Chevy II." Ahanu responded, "Oh man! That is a classic! Sorry, I thought it was a clunker." Joseph chuckled, "Well, all I had said was that it was an older car. I see you standing on the curb." Ahanu replied, "Oh yeah. I see your puke green car." The men were laughing as they hung up.

Joseph jumped out to open the trunk as he greeted Ahanu, "Great to see you, Ahanu!" Ahanu replied, "It is great to be seen!" As the men headed home, Joseph asked, "Do you want to go straight to my place, or do you want to take a drive?" Ahanu smiled, "I am up for whatever you'd like to do." Joseph smiled, "Alright. Let us take a drive on Highway 1, then head back home. I find the ocean is very relaxing."

Ahanu replied, "That's probably like my mountains make me feel."
Joseph replied, "Exactly!"

Joseph headed up to Malibu, making numerous stops along the way so
Ahanu could step on the beaches. Ahanu laughed, "I have never seen
such a beautiful sight. The water is breathtaking. I should get out of
Denver more often." Joseph responded, "You are always welcome
here. Have you ever had crab quesadillas?" Ahanu glanced over at his
friend, "Can't say that I have. Not sure it sounds good." Joseph
laughed, "That's what I thought before I had one. The first one I ever
had was in Avila Beach, about a three-hour drive from here. Shall we
grab a bite?" Ahanu chuckled, "Dude, I'm always hungry." Joseph
chuckled, "Well, you will have to learn to let me know because I don't
get hungry. I can sometimes go all day and finally realize I haven't
eaten." Ahanu responded, "Well, I will have to teach you to eat often.
I normally eat every three hours." Joseph chuckled, "I do too!"

Joseph pulled up into a parking lot of a restaurant. He asked, "Do you
like seafood?" Ahanu smiled, "If it is cooked, I can eat anything."
Joseph smiled, "Yeah, me too."

The men entered the restaurant and waited. The server walked
toward them and asked, "Is it two today?" Joseph smiled, "Yes. Just
the two of us." As they followed the server to their table, Joseph
asked, "May we be seated outside by the beach?" The server turned
and smiled, "It is very loud outside, but you're welcome to have a seat
out there." Joseph answered, "I am used to the sound of the waves.
My friend is from Denver. I think he will enjoy it." She led them out
and handed them menus. She asked, "May I get you started with
something to drink?" Joseph asked, "Do you have fresh-squeezed
lemonade?" She answered, "Sorry, we don't. Our lemonade is from
the soda fountain." Ahanu asked, "What do you recommend for a city
boy?" She smiled, "We do have a great Pina colada. We carry a variety
of soda products." Ahanu laughed, "I don't feel like a Pina colada, but
how about a root beer?" She replied, "We have that in a can, bottle,
or fountain drink. Do you have a preference?" Ahanu thought for a
moment. "How about a bottle." Joseph chuckled, "Make that two."

The young woman made eye contact with Joseph, "My name is Monica. If you have any questions about the menu, let me know." She smiled and walked away.

Ahanu laughed, "Did you see how she looked at you?" Joseph shyly smiled, "Not sure what you mean?" Ahanu replied, "Dude, I think she is into you." Joseph shook his head, "No. She probably thinks I am your little brother." The men laughed. Ahanu asked, "Tell me about your life. Because it sure is weird that we look so much alike." Joseph answered, "I am not sure where to start. How about we save that conversation for the house. Let's enjoy this atmosphere and the food." Ahanu answered, "Sounds good. So, what do you like here?" Joseph said, "It has been a while since I was here. I enjoy most any seafood. Although, salmon is my favorite." Ahanu replied, "I am used to the freshwater catches of Colorado. Many types of trout, Kokanee Salmon, and Mountain Whitefish. So, anything from the ocean is truly new to me." Joseph smiled, "Well, let's order a few dishes so you can try them out." Ahanu laughed, "Won't we look like pigs?" Joseph laughed, "No. You would be surprised how many people order like this. It's called family-style dishes."

Monica returned with their sodas. She asked, "I took the liberty to bring a couple of scoops of ice cream for your sodas. It is on the house. Have you made up your minds?" Joseph replied, "Thank you! It is very thoughtful of you. I do love my ice cream." Ahanu laughed, "I am not much of an ice cream fan, but I love floats." Joseph asked, "Do you want me to order?" Ahanu answered, "Yes. That would be good." Monica smiled, "Well, what looks good?" Joseph began, "Let's do oysters on the half shell, salmon, crab, and lobster." Monica smiled, "You must be hungry. That is quite a selection." Joseph added, "My friend is a mountain man, accustomed to freshwater seafood. He will enjoy this selection and experience." Monica smiled, "As you wish." She turned and walked away.

Joseph asked, "How was your flight? Anything unusual?" Ahanu chuckled, "There was something odd that happened. The flight was full, but somehow no one sat next to me. Although, strangely enough, it felt as if someone was sitting next to me." Joseph laughed, "Oh yeah? Tell me about it."

Ahanu smiled, "Well, I could feel the warmth of a person, but no one was next to me. It did not freak me out. Instead, I felt or sensed a wave of peace. I felt like the Creator was sitting next to me." Joseph asked, "Creator?" Ahanu smiled, "I am Native American. You know that, right?" Joseph laughed, "No. I don't know that we spoke about that." Ahanu laughed, "I think the last time we spoke was about what we did for a living and where we lived. Work and travel, you were going to Europe when I ran into you. So, we didn't get too deep into a conversation."

Joseph laughed, "Yeah, it was strange seeing you and feeling like I was looking at myself." Ahanu laughed, "Yeah, I thought I had a vision or memory of myself in my youth." As the men laughed, Monica arrived with the food.

As she placed the dishes on the table, she asked, "Is there anything else I can get?" Joseph asked, "May I please get a plate full of lemons. I like a lot of lemon on my seafood." Monica replied, "Of course! I will bring that right out."

Joseph asked, "So do you give thanks before eating?" Ahanu answered, "Yes, I do." Joseph asked, "Would you do the honor?" Ahanu answered, "It would be my pleasure. Creator of all things living and breathing. Thank you for your provision, for nourishing our bodies and souls. Thank you for Joseph and for this time of brotherhood. Amen."

Joseph asked, "So what would you like to try first?" Ahanu laughed, "It all looks delicious so just tell me what it is, and I will dig in." Joseph said, "These are the oysters on the half shell. Most people may tell you that adding nothing is better, but my experience suggests that you add a little lemon." Ahanu asked, "Why do they suggest nothing?" Joseph smiled, "Well, they want you to try it first to experience the taste. Personally, I prefer to add lemon." He laughed as he squeezed lemon on his. Ahanu was trying to decide. He answered, "Okay, I am going to get brave. I'm going in."

Joseph laughed, "Atta boy!" Ahanu laughed as he finished eating his first oyster. "That is just terrible! Why would you have let me eat it without anything?" Joseph laughed, "I tried to tell you." Ahanu grabbed a slice of lemon and ate it. "I think I will trust your recommendations from now on." Joseph responded, "These are my least favorite thing to eat." Ahanu asked, "Why did you order them?" Joseph smiled, "I want you to experience everything. Come on, mountain man, try another with lemon." Ahanu smiled and said, "No thanks. One of those is enough for me. What's next?" The men enjoyed the rest of their meal. Joseph explained what they were eating and made his recommendations.

Ahanu asked, "Why haven't we talked about your family?" Joseph replied, "I was adopted, and both my parents have passed away. So, I do have distant family, but I am not close to them. It's a long story." Ahanu said, "I see. Do you know anything about your birth parents?" Joseph paused, then replied, "I know my mom was very young. I know a little more, but I would rather talk about that when we get back to my place. Is that okay?" Ahanu answered, "Of course it is. We have a few days together, so there is no hurry."

Ahanu changed the subject, "Tell me about Europe? How are the women there?" Joseph chuckled, "Europe was great. Lots of work. We got a lot accomplished with the business I was consulting. I do not normally have a lot of time to go out. I focus on the assignment and work long hours." Ahanu teased, "How are you going to get married if you aren't going out?" Joseph replied, "I guess I will have to have you set me up." Joseph was laughing, then reversed the question, "How about you? Are you married?" Ahanu nodded his head, "Yes, I am. My wife is the best. Isabella is at home waiting to hear why you look like me. She thinks you are my twin from another mother and another decade." Ahanu was laughing. "I have a little girl too. Meekaila. She is a handful." Ahanu pulled out his wallet. "These are my girls."

Joseph smiled, "They are beautiful. Meekaila looks like her mommy." Ahanu replied, "Yes, she does." Joseph asked, "Are you planning on having more kids?" Ahanu shook his head, "No. We lost my son a few years ago, and it's hard." He pulled out another picture and handed it to Joseph. Joseph's heart broke as he looked at this little boy. "He is the spitting image of us. What happened?" Ahanu choked out, "We can talk about him another time." Joseph sympathetically replied, "I am so sorry for your loss."

They had finished eating, and Joseph stood up, "You ready to take a walk on the beach?" Ahanu smiled, "Yeah. That would be good."

The men walked to the beach in silence. Joseph was the first to speak, "I feel closer to the Creator here. The beach is calming, soothing, and helps me rest." Ahanu answered, "I feel peace here. I know the waves are powerful, but I feel at peace here. I think the girls would like it here." Joseph replied, "You can bring your family and come to stay with me any time you'd like." Ahanu replied, "Thanks. We will take you up on that for sure."

As the men reached the water, Ahanu asked, "Do you think we can go surfing? I mean, after you show me how to surf." Joseph laughed, "Yeah, dude. That is a priority of mine. I love to surf, so I was planning on it." Ahanu chuckled, "Of course, you can't tell Meekaila that I surfed. She was worried that the sharks were waiting to eat me." Joseph laughed, "No way, man. I will have to tell her all about sharks, so she isn't afraid of them." The men were deep in thought as they waded in the water.

After some time, the men headed back to the car. Joseph asked, "Do you want to drive further north or head home?" Ahanu replied, "Let's head home. We can go for a drive tomorrow." Joseph asked, "I forgot to ask, did you enjoy lunch?" Ahanu laughed, "Yeah, everything but the oysters." Joseph laughed, "That's how I feel about them too. Are you sure we are not twins?" The men laughed. Joseph asked, "Are you going to want to surf today? I tend to go out morning and night." Ahanu replied, "I am up for a lesson. I cannot wait to get in the water. Do you play beach volleyball?" Joseph answered, "I have played a little. I am not very good." Ahanu answered, "You don't have to be good to enjoy it." Joseph replied, "You don't know me. I must be good to enjoy anything. Maybe I should change my mindset on that."

Ahanu laughed, "Maybe that's an only child thing." Joseph laughed, "Maybe."

Ahanu added, "I used to be very competitive, but that changed when I had kids. They are such a beautiful blessing. It made me realize that winning or being the best at sports wasn't as important as being the best dad." Joseph replied, "I need to learn that from you before becoming a dad." Joseph continued, "So what sports did you enjoy before having kids?" Ahanu replied, "Who says I gave up sports?" Joseph teased, "I mean, you are pretty old, so I figured you could not participate." Ahanu laughed, "I am not as old as you think. I still play occasionally but would rather spend time with Meekaila." Joseph asked, "So what do you play?" Ahanu laughed, "Occasionally, I will play softball, volleyball, soccer, and flag football. A few years ago, I was very busy playing after work; however, when we lost Liam, I quit everything. I realized I did not spend enough time with him. It's in hindsight, but I don't want that for Meekaila."

Chapter 16 The View

Ahanu was in awe of the view as they arrived at Joseph's home. "Wow, you get to see this all time. Do you realize how blessed you are?" Joseph replied, "I do. I am gone so much that getting home is a respite. I enjoy the quiet." Ahanu replied, "You are not kidding. I love this view." Joseph added, "The sunsets are awesome. I like to sit out here and meditate on Yah's creative beauty. That is when I am not surfing."

The men headed inside to settle in. Joseph asked, "Do you want to grill tonight or go out?" Ahanu laughed, "My only request is no oysters!" Joseph asked, "Okay. Would you prefer burgers or fish?" Ahanu smiled, "Burgers are good. When are we eating?" Joseph smiled, "Oh yeah, I forgot you eat often. I will get the grill ready." Ahanu excused himself, "I will step out and call my girls."

Joseph had everything ready when Ahanu returned, "How do you like your burger?" Ahanu replied, "Medium." Ahanu was surprised that Joseph had everything ready. "Did I take too long with my girls?" Joseph replied, "No, I am used to grilling. I have everything in one place, so it's easy to pull things together."

The men sat to enjoy their burgers. As they spoke, Ahanu looked at Joseph and said, "I asked Isabella to inquire of family members to see if anyone may have given up a baby for adoption. I feel like you are my family. It's a feeling I haven't had about other people." Joseph was a little surprised, "I know we must be family. Two strangers shouldn't look this much alike." Ahanu asked, "Can you tell me what you know about your mom?" Joseph laughed, "Well, in the natural, all I knew was that I was abandoned in a trash receptacle. My mom died when I was seven then my dad when I was in high school. It was rough growing up with a dad that did not show me any affection. But then the Father came into my life, and that's who you see now." Ahanu responded, "I am sorry for your loss. It does not sound fun at all."

Joseph continued, "Don't feel bad. I am happier now than I ever was. Yah, the Creator, has been showing me a lot." Ahanu asked, "What do you mean?" Joseph began, "You believe in the Creator, right?" Ahanu replied, "Yes." Joseph asked, "Do you believe He speaks to us?" Ahanu answered, "Of course." Joseph continued, "Well, He gives me dreams and visions. Occasionally, I hear His voice, audibly." Ahanu replied, "Yeah, I believe He does." Joseph continued, "He has shown me my mother. She was very young, maybe about 14 or 15 years old. My mother was drinking, drugged, and raped at a party. She was alone and scared when she had me. She left me in her varsity athletic jacket in the trash receptacle. She watched from a short distance as the trash truck came to pick it up. Afterward, she left crying, and she told me she was sorry and that she loved me."

Joseph continued, "There is more but knowing that gave me peace. I could not blame her. She was just a child. In this vision, I heard Yah speak to me. He said, 'attah ben-yachiyd asher ahav, you are my beloved son whom I love. He told me my name was Yoceph. Then my mom named me Joseph." Ahanu laughed, "That is incredible!" Joseph chuckled, "Yeah, it is kind of cool. Most of this revelation, I received coming home from Europe." Ahanu said, "Wow. That is recent." Joseph responded, "Knowing the love of the Father is what transforms us." Ahanu smiled, "It is, isn't it?"

Ahanu asked, "What did your mom look like?" Joseph smiled, "Like me. She had dark straight hair - a beautiful big smile, and she was dark-skinned like me. Her eyes were very kind and seemed to twinkle. She had high cheekbones, long eyelashes, a kind face. She wore her eyebrows more natural. You know, not thinned out like many women of today, but they were not bushy either." Ahanu laughed, "I wish I were a profiler; maybe I could sketch what you're describing.' Joseph replied, "Me too. I can still see her. If I could sketch, I would have sketched her face. I look a lot like her."

Ahanu was in deep thought then responded, "She must be related to me. I haven't met all my relatives, but maybe we can do a DNA study to see who she may be." Joseph replied, "I have thought about that but am waiting for Creator to lead me. I believe if I try to do it on my own, the timing may be wrong." Ahanu replied, "Sometimes, we are supposed to do things when Creator prompts us with an idea." Joseph replied, "Possibly. But, you know, she would only be about 40 years old. That's young."

Ahanu asked, "Do you know anything about your biological father?" Joseph was jerked out of his thought, "No. What I saw in the spirit, my guess, is that he may have been a senior in High School or college age. He did look older than my mother did. He was tall, handsome, but it was hard to focus on him when I realized he was about to rape her." Ahanu asked, "Do you hate him for hurting and violating your mother?" Joseph replied, "No. I feel sorry that he felt that his behavior was acceptable. He allowed his hormones to lead. I asked the Creator to help me forgive him. I did not even notice what nationality he was. He is a blur to me." Ahanu replied, "Well, I am sure you will see his face when it's time. So clearly, your mother has Native American roots." Joseph asked, "Is it possible to look Native American yet not be?" Ahanu answered, "Sure, it could be that this gene is dominant in you. I believe you must have some Native American ancestry. Besides, I believe that we all came from one family at the beginning of time." Joseph replied, "I do too."

Ahanu asked again, "Would you be willing to do a DNA search? I would send my DNA too if you are willing?" Joseph thought for a moment, "I will have to pray about it. I appreciate your willingness to help."

Ahanu decided to change the subject, "My family is having a reunion in Colorado. I would love for you to come." Joseph asked, "Really? When?" Ahanu smiled, "It's in a couple of months. First, I will have Isabella send me the details. Then, I will add you as my guest." Joseph smiled, "That would be cool." Ahanu replied, "I feel you are my family. I can't shake the feeling of knowing you." Joseph replied, "I must be.

We do look like twins separated by a couple of decades." The men laughed.

Joseph was still thinking about the family reunion. He asked, "Have you ever seen any relative at the reunion that looks like you?" Ahanu smiled and laughed, "Yeah, everyone." Joseph's eyes opened wider with interest, "Do you think my mother may have been at these reunions?" Ahanu answered, "I must believe that she has or will. We look too much alike for her not to be there. Not everyone can make it every year. However, there must be a very high probability." Joseph replied, "If it is the Creator's Will, it will be done."

Ahanu asked, "Tell me what your trip was like coming home." Joseph smiled, "It was supernatural!" Ahanu laughed, "Do tell." Joseph continued, "It started with Creator asking me to change my flight. Then a young man, Timothy, sat next to me. He started a conversation, but I attempted to ignore him. By the way, when Creator ordains something, He means to finish it." Ahanu laughed, "I am starting to get goosebumps." Joseph continued, "I had multiple visions, dreams and experienced Ruach Haqodesh like never before." Ahanu asked, "Ruach Haqodesh?" Joseph answered, "Holy Spirit." Ahanu replied, "Oh, the Great Spirit." Joseph smiled, "Yes!" Ahanu added, "I have only experienced the Great Spirit at our gatherings." Joseph asked, "Do you know Creator on a personal level?" Ahanu smiled, "How personal?"

Joseph explained, "Do you know him as your Savior?" Ahanu replied, "I am not sure what you mean." Joseph asked, "What do you believe about Jesus Christ or, as I call Him, Yahushuah HaMashiach?" Ahanu answered, "He is the Son of God. I still don't understand what you mean by on a personal level." Joseph smiled, "Well, do you see Yahushuah HaMashiach as a friend? Do you see Creator as a Papa? Do you see Ruach Haqodesh as your comforter or teacher?"

Ahanu thought for a moment, "Yeah, I guess I do. I see Creator as Grandfather or Papa. Jesus is the White man's God and the One who gives us hope for redemption. The Great Spirit I see as the One that shows me things. So very similar to how you see Him. So, I do believe they are One. Three separate but One. I never thought of knowing them personally, but I guess I do." Joseph was nodding his head in agreement. Ahanu continued, "The Navajo call hozho 'the way of beauty,' where we live in harmony with all of the Creator's creation to enjoy the beauty, He has placed around us. The earth and the heavens above, alike. We say ikce wicasa, which means we are common human persons on the road. Jesus is the one that provides redemption. We are not as 'heathen' as the early settlers believed us to be."

Joseph chuckled, "I always want to know where people are, knowing who God is. You said you only experienced the Great Spirit at gatherings. I believe you should experience Him every day whether at home, work, or play." Ahanu asked, "How do you do that?" Joseph asked, "Can you tell me about your finding faith in the Father, Son, and Holy Spirit?" Ahanu smiled, "I know you are up to something, but I will play along." Joseph laughed, "No. I want to see how you came to know God the Creator." Ahanu began, "I knew of the Creator as a child but as the One who created everything except me. My father was misguided in telling me that he and mother were the ones that created me. Then he continuously told me how worthless I was. Then, I met Isabella, and she introduced me to God the Creator. I saw what a beautiful young woman she is inside and out. It was easy for me to believe that He had created her. I started going to church with her, and one thing led to another, I believe."

Joseph smiled, "That's cool, man." Ahanu smiled, "Yeah, you will love her when you meet her. She already loves you." Joseph smiled, "I love her too. I see that she has impacted you greatly. I am so grateful for that." Ahanu continued, "Isabella carries Creator's joy. It is infectious. Meekaila also carries an abundance of joy. I am very fortunate to have met Isabella." Joseph added, "I believe Creator had that ordained from the beginning of time. How well do you know the Word?" Ahanu smiled bashfully, "I am learning it. I cannot quote it like some do." Joseph replied, "You don't have to. Ruach Haqodesh helps you when you need to speak to someone. You must read the Bible or Torah." Ahanu confessed, "I have to be honest; I do not read much by myself, but Isabella makes sure we read together as a family in the evenings."

Joseph responded, "That's awesome! That's teaching Meekaila how important family time is."

Joseph asked, "Ahanu, have you ever been baptized?" Ahanu shook his head, "No. I haven't felt ready to do that." Joseph asked, "May I ask why?" Ahanu replied, "I believe in God. Isn't that enough?"

Joseph paused for a moment, then proceeded, "You see, the Word says that we need to believe that Jesus is the Son of God. Our faith in Jesus saves us from God's wrath. 'In John 14:6, Jesus said to him, "I am the [only] Way [to God] and the [real] Truth and the [real] Life; no one comes to the Father but through Me.' In Matthew 28:19, Jesus commanded his apostles to make disciples of all nations and to baptize people in the Name of the Father, the Son, and the Holy Spirit. Water baptism is our legal entrance into the Kingdom of God. We go from being a child of God to a Son of God. A Holy Spirit Baptism allows the Teacher to develop in us the Character of Christ, the Mashiach, so that our lives demonstrate the Power of the Kingdom of God." Ahanu asked, "So I should get baptized?" Joseph answered, "I believe you should. I do not think like most people. Many people believe that you must go to classes before being baptized. My way of thinking is that you believe in Jesus as the Son of God and your Messiah, confess your sins, and receive baptism by water and the Holy Spirit. It is important that you read the Bible. Then you rock and roll! If it can happen all in one day, the sooner, the better."

Ahanu thought for a moment, "I would love for my wife and daughter to be here, but I don't want to wait any longer. Can you baptize me?" Joseph smiled, "I would be honored to baptize you. Do you want to fly them in for this? I would love to meet them." Ahanu answered, "Isabella is working, and Meekaila is in school." Joseph smiled, "They could play hooky for a day. I can get their tickets by using some of my sky miles and get them here tonight. I can also call my new brother Timothy and have him bring his family as witnesses." Ahanu laughed, "Boy! You think fast on your feet. Let me call Isabella and make sure they can come down tonight." He stood up and walked out to make the call.

Joseph was searching for flights when Ahanu walked back in. Ahanu smiled, "Let's bring them down." Joseph asked, "How soon can they get to the airport? We could have them here by nine or ten." Ahanu laughed, "They are packing as we speak. It would be an hour before they would arrive at the airport." Joseph was excited, "Alright. Here are the details of the flight. I can email or text them to her." Ahanu said, "Send them by email. She can pull it up on her phone. You do not know how excited they are to meet you." Joseph smiled, "I am excited as well. My family keeps growing. Shall I call my brother Timothy?" Ahanu answered, "Yeah. The more, the merrier!"

Joseph called Timothy, "Hello Timothy. Do you remember I told you about Ahanu? Well, I am going to baptize him tomorrow. Can you and your sister come up for the day?" Timothy answered, "I would love that. I will check and see if Karen can. Oh, she says yes. She is over here eavesdropping." Joseph laughed, "I can't wait to see you all again. Tell Timmie that I will take her surfing."

Chapter 17 Baptism Day

Joseph snuck out of the house, quiet as a mouse. He had missed his evening surfing but was not about to miss his early morning surf despite going to bed late. Isabella and Meekaila were very tired from the long day. He was deep in thought as he raced to the water. 'Papa, thank You for this beautiful family You have put in my life. He heard Him answer, I love you, son. Papa, will I get to meet my natural mother? He heard His voice clearly; the things I have planned for you go beyond your comprehension. Do not limit me, son. Okay, Papa. I will keep my eyes open.'

The water was eerily calm. Joseph closed his eyes and faced the sky. Suddenly he heard a splash as he opened his eyes to a greeting by a school of dolphins. He laughed, "Have you come to play with me?" The dolphins seemed to respond to Joseph as they chattered and jumped around him. One appeared to be splashing him. Joseph laughed and splashed back. Then as suddenly as they appeared, they were gone. Joseph asked, 'Papa, did you send your little ones to make me laugh?' He heard, 'yes, son. I wanted to hear you laugh. Your laughter brings me joy.' Joseph asked, 'Am I going to be able to catch a good one?' He heard a laugh, 'Speak to the wave to form.' Joseph looked around. 'Wave, form. I want to surf.' Suddenly he felt it. It was a big one. As he caught the wave, he laughed and shouted. 'Thank you, Papa!'

He headed in to prepare breakfast for his guests. The house was quiet and darkened. He snuck into the kitchen and began to take out breakfast items. First, he decided to cut up some fruit. He had oranges, strawberries, and watermelon. Then, he thought to himself, 'pancakes or French toast? Not everyone likes French toast, so I better go with pancakes.' As the aromas of breakfast traveled through the house, he heard the guest bedroom door open. It was Meekaila. She said, "Good morning, Joseph! You are a good cook. Everything smells so good." Joseph smiled, "Good morning Meekaila. Did you sleep well?" Meekaila answered, "Oh yeah. The bed was very comfortable. I slept all night long. I usually wake up during the night."

Joseph smiled, "Oh really? Why do you wake up?" Meekaila answered, "I don't know. Sometimes I hear noises, and sometimes it is a bad dream." Joseph asked, "I know I should not ask a young lady this question, but how old are you?" Meekaila laughed, "You can ask me that because I am not a lady yet." Joseph laughed, "Ok. How old are you?" Meekaila smiled, "I am seven years old. I am in second grade, and my teacher's name is Miss Worthy." Joseph replied, "Well, Meekaila. That makes you old enough to help me with breakfast. Would you like to help?" Meekaila's eyes brightened up, "Oh yes, please. I would love to help." Joseph instructed her, "If you could get some syrup out of the pantry, we can set the table afterward." She opened the pantry and laughed, "You have everything organized. Mommy does not have her pantry like yours." Joseph answered, "Well, it's a little easier when you are only one person that puts things away. I am sure you and daddy help mommy, right?" She laughed, "I guess so. I know why you are nice to me." Joseph laughed, "Alright, Miss Smarty Pants. Did you find the syrup?" Meekaila answered, "Yes, sir. Can I get some chocolate chips for my pancakes?" Joseph smiled, "You may have anything you would like. Hope mommy and daddy agree."

Ahanu answered, "She will have grace. We are at her uncle's house, and what he says goes." Meekaila ran to her daddy, "Good morning, daddy! I tried not to wake you and mommy. Did you sleep well?" Ahanu answered, "I sure did. I had the best sleep I have had in quite a while." Joseph replied, "Oh, good to hear that. I always wonder if that bed is comfortable." Ahanu answered, "Good morning, Joseph. You know you did not have to do this. We could have gone out for breakfast." Joseph answered, "I know. I wanted to." They smiled at each other.

Meekaila asked, "Is mommy awake?" Ahanu replied, "Yes. She is getting ready." Meekaila laughed and turned to Joseph, "That is code, for it will be a little while." Ahanu laughed, "No. Today she is hurrying up. She could smell the wonderful aroma seeping into the room." Meekaila squealed with joy, "Yay!" Joseph laughed.

Ahanu added, "Yes. Today will be an unforgettable day." Meekaila asked, "Why daddy?" He answered, "First of all, I am getting baptized and will be God's Son. Then, we get to spend time with Joseph as a family. We also are meeting his friend and brother Timothy." Meekaila was jumping up and down. She squealed, "Oh yay! So, Timothy is going to be my uncle too?" Joseph answered, "Yes, of course!" Meekaila squealed, "I love having more uncles!" Isabella walked into the kitchen and asked, "What is all this joy about?" Meekaila answered, "I am going to have another uncle!" Isabella laughed.

Joseph added, "Speaking of uncles. Timothy, his sister Karen, and niece Timmie should be arriving between 10 and 11. We could do lunch then hit the water. How does that sound?" Isabella answered, "That sounds good to me." Meekaila said, "Me too." Ahanu replied, "I was hoping to get baptized first. But you never know when we will meet our Creator, so I need to be prepared." Joseph chuckled, "Then baptism first. All right, let us sit down for breakfast. Meekaila, want to get the plates?" Meekaila ran to help Joseph. Isabella and Ahanu also assisted in carrying food to the table.

As they sat down, Joseph asked, "Meekaila, would you like to say grace?" Meekaila's eyes lit up, "Oh yes, please." Joseph nodded his head, "Please do the honors." Meekaila bowed her head, "Dear Jesus, thank You for my uncle, Joseph. Thank You for mommy and daddy. Thank you for bringing us to daddy's baptism. Thank you for this delicious breakfast. Please let all the little children of the world have food today. In Jesus' name, amen." Joseph smiled at her and then looked at Ahanu. "Papa answers all our prayers. Papa, please join us for breakfast." Meekaila started giggling. Ahanu asked, "What's so funny?" Meekaila replied, "I just feel so happy." Joseph added with a chuckle, "She is feeling the Creator's presence. His joy sometimes is so heavy that we giggle like children." Isabella was giggling. Ahanu said, "I don't feel anything." Joseph said, "Don't fight it because it seems silly. Just allow Creator to touch your heart." Ahanu placed his arms to his side and said, "Okay, Creator. Here I am." He had not finished speaking those words when he started giggling. It was as if he were a child again.

Breakfast was difficult to get through due to all the giggling. The harder everyone seemed to gather themselves to eat, the harder they giggled. Finally, as the group finished breakfast, a knock on the door. Joseph yelled, "Timothy come on in." The door opened, and Timothy peeked in his head. "What is going on in here?" He asked with a giggle. Suddenly everyone started giggling again. Timothy, Karen, and Timmie walked in giggling. Timmie ran to her uncle and jumped on him. She laughed, "Oh, Uncle Joey. I am so happy to see you!"

Joseph gathered himself and attempted introductions, "Please let me introduce you to my brother Timothy." Joseph burst out in laughter. "This is Timmie. Karen." Joseph could stop laughing. Ahanu smiled and took over the introductions. "I am Joseph's twin, Ahanu." Everyone laughed, "This is my wife, Isabella, and my daughter, Meekaila." Timmie climbed down from Joseph's arms, went, and hugged Meekaila. "You can be my sister!" Meekaila replied, "I love you, little sister!"

Once the Spirit of Joy subsided, they sat in the living room. Timothy smiled, "I see why you guys hit it off. You look so much alike." Ahanu responded, "So who do you think is more handsome?" Timothy laughed. Timmie answered, "You are both handsome." Everyone laughed.

Timmie asked impatiently, "When are we going to get in the water?" Joseph laughed, "Well, let's talk about a few things first, then we can baptize Ahanu." Timmie asked impatiently, "Ok, but when are we going surfing?" Joseph smiled at her, "after Ahanu's baptism. Then, I will give you a lesson." Timmie squealed with joy. "Yay!"

Joseph began, "I want to warn you. The water may be a little cold, especially without wetsuits. The waves are not too rough right now. If you go into the water, be careful not to go too far. If a big wave comes in, just steady yourself, stay balanced, and ride it in. I will bring my surfboards out for anyone who would like to surf or like a lesson. I have many towels, so we can each grab one or two. Whatever you like. Any questions?"

Timmie was the first to speak, "Can I go deep with you?" Joseph glanced over at Karen, "You need to ask your mom." Karen answered, "I trust Joseph. He can use his discernment." Joseph smiled at Karen. "I will take good care of her." Karen replied, "I know you will." Ahanu asked, "Are we ready? I know I am."

They headed out the door with beach towels under everyone's arms. The two girls ran ahead of the adults. As they reached the water's edge, the girls let out a squeal and jumped. Joseph had been watching them closely. "What do you see?" Timmie picked up a seashell and ran back to him. "Look, isn't this the prettiest seashell you have ever seen?" Joseph agreed, "Yes, it is. Look at all the pretty colors."

The adults put down the blankets when Ahanu said, "Let's do this. I am so ready!" Joseph asked, "Who is staying on the beach or coming closer?" Isabella and Karen were walking to the edge of the water. Karen answered, "We will stay here." Timothy said, "I will come in with you both." Joseph instructed the girls, "You stay here until after Ahanu is baptized. If you want to sing a song, go ahead."

The men walked out into the ocean. The water was just above their waist when they stopped. Joseph asked Ahanu, "Have you confessed your sins?" Ahanu smiled, "Yes, I have." Next, Joseph asked, "Have you received Yahushuah HaMashiach as your Lord and Savior?" Ahanu answered, "Yes, I have." Finally, Joseph asked, "Is it your choice to be baptized before these witnesses?" Ahanu answered, "Yes, as witnesses, in front of my family."

Joseph stated, "Ahanu, be baptized in the name of the Father, the Son, and Holy Spirit." Ahanu dipped himself into the water; Joseph said, "Ahanu receive your freedom." Ahanu came back up, smiling from ear to ear. They headed back to the shore. They saw all the women screaming and jumping. They heard, "Look up, look up!" The men looked up, and the clouds were in the form of angels blowing shofars. The men began to laugh. Ahanu ran to his wife and hugged her. He began to cry, "It was the most beautiful experience I have ever had."

Meekaila ran to Joseph, "I want to be baptized too." Joseph smiled and said, "Go tell mommy and daddy." Meekaila ran to her parents, "I want to be baptized too." Ahanu picked her up and headed out to Joseph. "Let's do this." Joseph said, "Ok, daddy. You know what to do." Ahanu asked, "Don't I have to be a minister or something?" Joseph laughed, "I am not a minister. Anyone can do this. Now that you have experienced this, you are qualified." Isabella came out to the men and Meekaila, "I also want to be baptized. My first baptism was when I was a child, maybe age five. Creator has put it on my heart to get baptized now." Joseph smiled, "Let's do it."

Ahanu asked, "Who wants to go first?" Isabella answered, "I should go first so I can help you baptize Meekaila." Ahanu smiled, "Okay." He asked, "Isabella, have you received Jesus as your Lord and Savior?" Isabella answered, "Yes." He asked, "Have you confessed your sins and asked for forgiveness?" She replied, "Yes." Ahanu continued, "Isabella, be baptized in the name of the Father, the Son, and Holy Spirit." She leaned back to allow herself to become fully immersed in water. Ahanu brought her back up. He hugged his wife.

Joseph smiled, "ok, Meekaila. Are you ready?" She shook her head and said, "Yes!" He walked her to her parents. He handed her to them. Isabella asked, "Do you want me or daddy to baptize you?" Meekaila laughed, "I want you both to do it together." Then, they asked in unison, "Meekaila, have you asked Jesus into your heart as Lord and Savior?" Meekaila answered, "Yes, when I was four." They continued, "Did you ask Jesus to forgive you for anything you did wrong?" Meekaila answered, "Yes, I did. He said I forgive you." They laughed and continued, "Meekaila, be baptized in the Name of the Father, the Son, and Holy Spirit." She plugged her nose, and they immersed her fully. She came out of the water with a squeal.

Timmie was cheering for her family. When they all arrived on the beach, Timmie asked, "Can we surf now?" Joseph grabbed his board and said, "Let's go, Timmie." Everyone watched as Joseph placed Timmie on his board and walked out.

Joseph asked, "Are you ready?" Timmie yelled, "Oh yeah! I have been waiting for this Uncle Joey." Joseph replied, "I will run beside you for the first couple of times, then let you go on your own. Okay?" Timmie answered, "Okay, Uncle Joey." Joseph saw a wave coming and yelled, "Here we go!" He ran beside the board, holding her so she would not wipe out. Timmie was screaming with joy. "This is so much fun!" Timmie surfed a few more times, with Joseph assisting her. Joseph asked, "Are you ready?" Timmie said, "Yes, sir!"

Joseph yelled, "Here she comes!" Timmie counted, "Ready, set, up." She stood up and screamed with joy as Joseph guided her. She rode the wave to the beach; Timmie screamed with joy and excitement. Karen ran to her, "You did it! You are an awesome surfer!" Joseph was laughing, "Why did you scream?" Timmie replied, "I was having so much fun and could not hold in my joy!"

Timmie looked at Meekaila, "You have to try this. Surfing is so much fun!" Meekaila laughed, "I want Uncle Joey to show me too." Joseph laughed, "Let's go!" He did the same thing with Meekaila. Timmie was on the beach cheering her on.

The men then took a turn surfing. Joseph gave them instructions, and off they went. They were quick learners. Once everyone had finished surfing. They headed in for lunch.

Everyone was lending a hand in preparing lunch; they worked together as if it was a regular thing and had been doing it for years. The little ones set the table. Once the burger and dogs were ready. Everyone sat down to enjoy the meal. Then, they started sharing their experience of the baptisms. Meekaila shared first, "I felt like I went to heaven. When I was underwater, I could see many colors. They were very bright neon colors. They were moving like waves. Did I stay underwater for a long time?" Ahanu answered, "No, honey. It was very fast." Meekaila laughed, "I thought I was underwater for a long time." Ahanu replied, "I felt the same way. I saw myself floating in bright light. I believe it was white. It was warm. I know the ocean is cold, but I felt warm, at peace, and amazing." Isabella shared, "I saw myself falling into a pool of Jesus' blood; when I came out, I was white as snow. I, too, felt like I had been doing it for a long time. I felt at peace. I also felt that I was so light, like a feather, similar to the sense of floating. I do not know how to explain it. Once I turned white, I was face down, flying all over the world."

Timmie shared, "When Uncle Ahanu was baptized. I saw many people celebrating in heaven. I also saw the angels dancing and praising God. Jesus was very happy."

Joseph was next to speak, "I love how we all have a different experience; each so unique." They continued to enjoy their visit. Suddenly the sun was setting. Joseph asked, "Timothy, will you be staying the night?" Timothy replied, "It is getting late. Sis, do you want to drive home?" Timmie replied, "I want to stay with Uncle Joey. Please, mommy?" Karen smiled, "Okay, it's a good thing we have a change of clothes."

Isabella added, "Joseph, if it's okay. We want to stay longer too. Maybe I can play hooky this once." Joseph laughed, "You are all welcome to stay as long as you like. Monday, I do have an appointment. However, mi casa es tu casa."

Joseph brought out the blow-up mattress for Karen and Timmie. Timothy was going to crash in Joseph's room. As everyone settled in for the night, Joseph teased, "Good night, John Boy." Ahanu replied, "Goodnight, Jim Bob.' Timmie giggled, "Goodnight, mama."

Chapter 18 Joey

Joseph was settling down in his seat. He had had a great visit with his new family. His trip to Phoenix to Mr. Paul Jones' business had been a success. He saw that the employees were all eager to learn something new. He saw a change in attitudes, and the business production improved. He could not have expected such a difference in just a few weeks. Joseph knew it was all from Heaven. He thought, 'Thank You, Yah, for sending me. I will go wherever you send me.'

Suddenly, he saw a familiar face. He smiled, "Hello, Lucy. How have you been?" Lucy was grinning, "I have been fantastic. Thank you for asking. It is a pleasure to see you on my flight. How have you been?" Joseph laughed, "I truly have no complaints. I am quite blessed. How do I have the pleasure of seeing you on a domestic flight?" Lucy laughed, "I moved to Denver a week ago. I felt I needed to be closer to my mom. I need to get back to my responsibilities, although I will be checking back in with you." Joseph added, "Well, this is a blessing. Do you think we could chat when we get to Denver?" Lucy smiled, "Yes, I was hoping you could take a few minutes once we land. Maybe I could show you around?" Joseph smiled, "That would be nice. I can make arrangements to have some time available." Lucy leaned over and whispered, "Should we expect another supernatural flight?" Joseph chuckled, "Let us see what Yah has planned." Lucy giggled and walked away.

Joseph laughed to himself. He was looking out the window when someone sat next to him. He turned and smiled; it was a small child. Joseph introduced himself, "Hi. My name is Joseph. How are you?" The little boy smiled, "That's my name too." Joseph smiled, "It is nice to meet you, Joseph." The boy smiled back, "You can call me Joey." Joseph asked, "Joey, are you traveling with your parents?" Joey replied, "No. My mom is waiting for me in Denver. My dad brought me to the airport." Joseph answered, "I see. How old are you?" Joey replied, "I am seven. How old are you?" Joseph chuckled, "I am 26." Joey asked, "Are you married?" Joseph smiled, "No, I am not. Someday I will get married." Joey said, "When you do, be nice to your son and wife." Joseph looked at Joey, "Is your dad nice to you?" Joey answered, "Sometimes. He is not nice to mommy. That makes me sad." Joseph was sympathetic to his pain and replied, "I am so sorry to hear that is happening to your mommy. Do you live with your mommy?" Joey replied, "Yes, I do. I only go to see daddy twice a year. He has another wife and kids too." Joseph smiled at him, "Well, that means that you have siblings. Are they nice to you?" Joey looked at Joseph, "No. They hate me." Joseph was shocked to hear that. "Why do you say they hate you?" He asked Joey. Joey answered, "Because that's what they say. Sometimes they punch and kick me. When I go to tell daddy, he spanks me for lying." Joseph felt himself getting angry. He asked, "So he does not believe you?" Joey started to cry, "I am not a liar. I tell the truth. He says I lie because his kids don't lie." Joseph asked, "Can I put my arm around you?" Joey nodded his head yes. Joseph spoke softly, "I am so sorry your daddy does not believe you. I believe you. Do you know who Jesus is?"

Joey shook his head yes. Joseph continued, "Jesus believes you. He is always with you. Do you know that?" Joey smiled, "Yes. I do know that. He is the one that told me not to worry but to pray for them all." Joseph smiled, "You are one brave boy and very smart. Do you know that?" Joey looked at Joseph, puzzled, "How am I brave? I cry when they hit me." Joseph answered, "To be brave does not mean that you do not cry. It means that you can face problems or danger without showing fear." Joey answered, "Oh, I see. I am not afraid when they are hitting me or being mean. I do stand up for myself." Joseph smiled, "Yes. You are brave and courageous. Also, you love them, so you forgive them and pray for them." Joseph added, "They must be jealous or afraid of you." Then, Joey was in deep thought and answered, "I think they are afraid of me. I told them that Jesus was going to be mad at them because they are so mean to me."

Joseph answered, "That's good." Joey continued, "My brother, who is bigger than me, pushed me and said I was stupid. I told him that I was a super-smart student. He laughed at me." Joseph continued to encourage him, "That is awesome that you told him you are super smart." Joey kept going, "My daddy said that my mommy was dumb. I told him that my mommy was not dumb. She works for the college and is a professor." Joseph responded, "Whoa." Joey continued, "I will tell my mommy that I do not want to go see daddy again. I am going to tell the judge not to make me go. I know my daddy does not love me like he loves his other kids."

Joseph was listening, "I see." Joey continued, "I will be praying for them because I do not want anything bad to happen to them. However, I do not want to go back. I leave my mommy all alone. I miss her when I leave." Joseph continued to reassure him, "I bet you do." Joey smiled at Joseph, "You are very nice. Where are you going?" Joseph smiled, "I am going to a family reunion." Joey asked, "Is your mommy going to be there?" Joseph smiled, "I hope so. I have never met her." Joey's eyes opened wide, "Did she get lost?" Joseph smiled, "Kind of; I think we both got lost." Joey asked, "How did you get lost?" Joseph laughed, "Well, she had to give me up for adoption when I was born." Joey replied, "Oh, I see. Daddy wanted mommy to give me up for adoption too, but mommy said no." Joseph said, "Joey, you and I are so much alike." Joey smiled, "I think so too. When I sat down, I imagined that I was traveling through time, and you were me all grown up." Joseph laughed, "Joey, you have a good imagination. What other things do you like to imagine?"

Lucy apologized, "I am so sorry to interrupt, but I want to see if you gentlemen would like something to drink." Joseph answered first, "I would like a root beer float." Joey quickly replied, "Me too!" Lucy laughed, "I wish I could get one for you, but we do not have ice cream on this flight. Can I bring you just the root beer?" Both Josephs nodded their heads and spoke in unison, "Sure." Joey began to laugh, "I think you are me in the future. You said the same thing." Joseph laughed, "I think you must be me in the past." The two continue to laugh.

Joey spoke, "You are very nice. I do not know any men that are as nice as you." Joseph asked, "Really? Isn't your grandpa nice?" Joey answered, "No. He is very mean. He does not want me and mommy to come over to his house. Grandma is very sad, and sometimes she comes alone to see us." Joseph replied, "I see. That must be very hard for you?" Joey smiled, "Not really. It has always been like that, so it doesn't bother me anymore."

Joseph decided to change the subject, "So before Lucy came to take our drink order, I asked you what other things you like to imagine?" Joey laughed, "I imagine someday that I will have a daddy. He is going to be very nice, like you. He is going to treat my mommy like a princess. He is going to love me like his son." Joseph encouraged him, "What do you think he will look like?" Joey smiled, "I would like him to have crazy hair. Maybe rainbow or blue. His eyes will be blue. And he will have a very nice smile." Joseph laughed, "Rainbow hair?" Joey replied, "Yes. This way, I will know it is him. I won't look in a crowd and lose him." Joseph was still laughing, "I see."

Joey continued, "He would like to eat ice cream and go to the park. He will want to ride bikes with mommy and me." Joseph egged him on, "What kind of car will he drive?" Joey continued, "He will have a sports car. Maybe a red one. To drive my mommy around." Joseph was laughing hard. Joey continued, "He will also need to have a safe car for me. I cannot go in sports cars. I am too little. But when I get bigger, he will give me the sports car."

Passengers had taken notice of little Joey's story and were also laughing. Joey was enjoying all the attention. He continued, "I also want a baby brother. Maybe a baby sister too. I promise to be a nice big brother." Joseph smiled at Joey, "I know you will be the best big brother." Joey nodded his head, "I will hug them and kiss them all the time. I will never punch them." Joseph said, "That will be very nice." Then he asked, "What else do you like to imagine?" Joey smiled, "I imagine I have a unicorn and a dinosaur." Joseph asked, "Really? Where would they live?" Joey answered, "Well, when I have my new daddy. We will have a big ranch. That's where we will all live."

Joseph replied, "I see. What will the unicorn and dinosaur eat?" Joey answered, "I think I will feed them ice cream. Sometimes maybe I will give them grass. Sometimes, maybe I will give them food from my plate. Or maybe they can sit at the table with us." Joseph smiled, "That will have to be a big table." Joey laughed, "No, silly. We will have one in the barn so we can eat together." Joseph laughed, "Of course. Why didn't I think of that? What color do you think your dinosaur will be?" Joey thought for a moment, "Well, I think it will be orange. That way, it will not get lost in the meadow." Joseph was smiling, "I see. What about your unicorn?" Joey was ready for that question, "All unicorns are white. They are from Heaven and have horns that are made of many colors. Not like a rainbow but many colors changing all the time." Joseph asked, "Really? What sound does it make in Heaven?"

Time had flown by for them both. Finally, Lucy asked, "Can you please buckle your seatbelts? We are getting ready to land. Joey, you have been so good on this flight, much better than most kids who travel. I have a special gift for you." She handed him a small box.

Joey smiled, "Thank you so much! I have never gotten a special gift before." Joseph smiled at Lucy, "Joey, open it. Let's see what you got." Joey opened the box. He started laughing as he peeked inside. He said, "I love it!" He pulled out a tiny dinosaur. He faced Joseph, "Is it okay if I name him Joseph? This way, I will always remember you." Joseph smiled, "Wow! That would be great. Thank you so much. You are my new friend." Joseph reached into his briefcase and pulled out a card. As he handed Joey his card, "This is my number. If you and your mommy ever need help. Please call me. Okay?" Joey smiled, "Is this your number?" Joseph replied, "Yes, it is." Joey smiled, "I have never had a best friend that is grown up. I will tell mommy all about you."

Lucy came by one last time to check Joey's seatbelt. "Joey, you have been such a great traveler. I will be the one taking you to find your mommy. Is that okay?" Joey answered, "Yes. You are my favorite helper. My mommy will like that you are taking me to her."

Lucy smiled at Joseph, "I will take Joey down to retrieve his luggage and meet his mom. Maybe we can meet there?" Joseph replied, "That sounds like a plan."

Joseph exited the plane and headed to the luggage claim. Joseph was not accustomed to picking up luggage. However, he had a sense of excitement for this trip. Joseph had told Ahanu that he would get a car and drive to his home. Before meeting up with Ahanu, he knew that Lucy's visit would be significant. Joseph stood at the baggage claim, carefully watching for his luggage. He suddenly noticed Lucy and Joey standing on the opposite side of the carousel, so he walked toward them and caught sight of his luggage. He first went around and grabbed his bag, then headed to them.

Joseph teased Joey, "Excuse me. You look very familiar. Have I met you before?" Joey laughed, "Yes, you have. Don't you remember me, Joseph?" Joseph laughed and winked at Lucy. "No, what is your name?" Joey giggled, "Remember? We are the same person, but you are from the future." Joseph laughed, "Oh, you must be me when I was younger. Are you Joey?" Joey continued to giggle. "Joseph, you are so funny! I wish I could take you home with me." Joseph smiled, "You could take Miss Lucy with you." Joey smiled at Lucy, "I think mommy would like to have a sister like you." Lucy laughed, "I sure would like to have a sister too."

Just then, Joey saw his mommy. Joey screamed out, "Mommy! Mommy!" Lucy followed close beside him. She introduced herself, "Hello, I am Lucy. I am the attendant in charge of Joey." Joey's mom introduced herself, "Hello. I am Sophia. Thank you for taking care of my boy." Lucy smiled, "He was a pleasure to have on my flight. He made friends quickly." Sophia asked, "Really? He doesn't seem to make friends very easily." Lucy explained, "Well, he had a very nice man sitting next to him. They talked the entire trip." Sophia looked worried, "I do not understand. I thought he was to be next to you?" Lucy explained, "He was. I had him in first class. Let me introduce you to Joseph." Joseph smiled, "Hello, Sophia. Joey is a mighty fine boy." Sophia looked at Joey, "Yes, he is. I hope he did not bother you."

Joseph reassured her, "He is a special young man. We talked about God, his father, and his siblings."

Sophia looked at Joseph and asked, "What did he say?" Joseph looked at Joey, "He said he was praying for them." Joey smiled, "Mommy, I do not want to go back to see daddy. I can tell the judge I do not want to go back." Sophia looked worried, "Are you okay? What happened?" Joey answered, "Mommy, do not worry. God watches over me all the time."

Joseph smiled at Sophia, "I hope it is okay, but I gave Joey my business card. If you ever need anything, please do not hesitate to call me." Sophia asked, "Why would we need your help?" Joseph responded, "I know you do not know me. Joey and I have much in common. I am a stranger that would be willing to help any way I can." Joey interrupted, "Mommy. Joseph is like an angel. I see him." Sophia smiled at her son, "I love you, baby. We can talk about this at home. Is that okay?" Joey responded, "Joseph is my best friend now. Jesus told me that I could trust him." Sophia was feeling uncomfortable. "Listen, I know my little boy must seem unusual, but he is a very good boy." Joseph smiled at Lucy, "Lucy, do I seem like an unusual guy?"

Lucy laughed, "Yes. I have never met another man like you." Joseph explained, "I lived a difficult life, and I am very blessed. God watches over me and sends me people to help. I believe that is why I met Joey." Sophia was surprised, "I do not understand. What do you mean?" Joseph explained, "Listen. Joey has a special gift of seeing angels and Heaven. I am somewhat similar. God speaks to me in unusual ways. Your son has a powerful God connection." Sophia smiled, "Yes, he does. You are the first man he has trusted. I believe him. It is just difficult to trust." Joseph answered, "I understand. I am not pushy, and you can take all the time you need to get to know who I am. I mean absolutely no harm to Joey. He has a special name."

Sophia spotted the luggage, and immediately Joey ran to it. Joseph followed Joey and removed the bags off the conveyor belt. Sophia said, "Thank you for your kindness toward my Joey. He does need a man in his life that is positive." Joseph laughed, "Yes, he has an idea of what that man will be like."

Joey hugged Joseph, "Thank you for being my new best friend. I know we will call you to talk." Sophia added, "I will keep your card. If it is okay, I can have Joey call you." Joseph smiled, "That would be just fine. I live in California, but you can call anytime."

They said their goodbyes and went on their way. Joseph perceived that they would become good friends.

Chapter 19 Dessert

Lucy and Joseph headed to a cafe. Joseph asked, "Are you hungry?" Lucy smiled, "No, I am not hungry. Although, I would have some dessert." Joseph responded, "That sounds good to me too."

As they stood in line, they joked about the desserts. Joseph teased, "So if you were a dessert, what would you be?" Lucy thought and then answered, "I would be German Chocolate Cake." Joseph asked, "Is that because the coconut is fun and exciting with a little nuttiness too?" Lucy laughed, "NO! It has a smooth chocolate flavor; the coconut makes it tropical, and you must have nuts on most everything." Joseph laughed, "I like my description much better."

Lucy asked, "Okay, smarty pants. What kind of dessert would you be?" Joseph challenged Lucy, "What if I give you the description, and you guess what I would be?" Lucy replied, "That sounds interesting." Joseph explained, "I am all American. I would be in your eye. I would also have a friend with me, maybe two. What am I?" Lucy laughed, "I have no idea." Joseph encouraged her and added, "I would hit it out of the ballpark. Does that help?" Lucy was laughing, "You're a baseball?" Joseph laughed, "NO! It's a dessert." Lucy repeated the clues, "Okay, okay, let me try. You are all American. You would be in my eye. You might have a friend or two. You are something about a ballpark. You are a dessert hot dog!" Joseph laughed, "I have never heard of one! Let me give you another clue. My friend or friends would be creamy smooth." Lucy laughed, "Okay, that could be ice cream." Joseph laughed. Lucy thought some more, "Something with ice cream." Joseph laughed, "Yes!" Lucy spoke out, "Something about my eye. You are the sparkle of my eye. You are the light of my eye. You are the apple of my eye." Joseph was grinning. Lucy laughed, "Yes! The apple of my eye! Okay, let's see. Apple and ice cream. Apple pie and ice cream!" Joseph high-fived her. Joseph said, "Good job!" They had passed the time in line, and now it was time to order.

He looked at Lucy, "What would you like?" Lucy laughed, "I didn't look at the menu." Joseph asked, "Do you mind if I order first as you decide?" Lucy laughed, "Of course that's okay!" Joseph smiled at the young man and placed his order, "I will have a slice of Coconut Cake and a scoop of vanilla ice cream." Lucy smiled at Joseph, "That sounds delicious!" Joseph smiled, "You are welcome to taste mine if you like." Lucy laughed, "I cannot decide, so I will have a slice of German Chocolate Cake and a slice of Coconut Lemon Cake. May I also please have a glass of milk?" The young man asked, "Will these orders be on separate checks?" Joseph answered, "No. One check is fine. Thank you." Lucy asked, "Shall I give you cash for my order, or can we just split it in half?" Joseph smiled, "Please allow me to treat you." Lucy smiled, "Okay but do not make this a habit." Joseph replied, "Oh, I promise to make it a habit." They both laughed. Joseph paid and received a number.

They headed to a table and sat down. Joseph was the first to speak, "So, tell me what has been going on in your life since we last saw each other?" Lucy smiled, "I have had so many supernatural things happening since I saw you last. I started seeing in the spirit. I had never experienced that before." Joseph asked, "What have you seen?" Lucy answered, "I am seeing angels. I believe they are the guardian angels of people." Joseph asked, "Do tell. Do they give you a message for the people?" Lucy responded, "No. When I see them, I understand what each person's calling is, and sometimes, I find I have a prophetic word for them." Joseph replied, "That is awesome. What else have you experienced?" Lucy smiled, "I also have started to dream in Hebrew. I do not speak a word of Hebrew, but I see the lettering and understand it in English." Joseph smiled, "That is cool."

Lucy suddenly was very serious. "Joseph, from the moment I met you, I knew you were special. But now, I see how special you are." Joseph was confused, "I don't understand?" Lucy continued, "I see your guardian angels. They are massive. They look like warriors." Joseph sat back and thought for a moment. Then, he asked her, "Are you allowed to tell me what they look like?" Lucy hesitated, "All I can say is that they look like Native American warriors. They are huge. Maybe like chiefs. They have a headdress on." Joseph replied, "I see. That does answer a few things for me."

Joseph asked, "Did I tell you that I am headed to a family reunion?" Lucy smiled, "No. I just knew you were meeting a friend." Joseph explained, "I am headed to my first family reunion ever. I am super excited to be meeting these people." Lucy asked, "How long will you be in town?" Joseph smiled, "Well, I haven't figured that out yet. I have three weeks off. I guess it depends on how it goes at the reunion." Lucy laughed, "They are going to love you!" Joseph replied, "I sure hope so. I am hoping to meet my mother for the first time." Lucy replied, "That is great news!" Joseph laughed, "Yeah, if it happens. Not my will, but God's will be done." Lucy asked, "So you must be adopted?" Joseph smiled, "Yes, I was. I met a man that looks so much like me. I feel this is a God thing." Lucy laughed, "I will be praying for you. Joseph, I know God has many exciting plans for you." Joseph smiled, "I think so too. I only got a one-way ticket here until I see when I am to head out."

Joseph shifted the conversation, "Tell me about your mom." Lucy smiled, "Well, she is getting older, and I am her only child. I have been away from home for a very long time. I put my career before my parents. Daddy went to heaven a few years back, and my mom needs help with everything. Therefore, I thought it was a good time to make a change. I am closer to home with domestic flights. I still travel all the time, but I am much closer." Joseph asked, "Is she ill?" Lucy replied, "No, just elderly." Joseph asked, "You don't look very old, so it's hard to imagine your mom as elderly." Lucy laughed, "Well, they adopted me late in life."

Just then, the desserts arrived. Joseph laughed, "Oh my. These are huge servings." Lucy also laughed, "How in the world am I going to finish both of these?" Joseph chuckled, "You know, there is a Christian comedian that makes fun of prayer for appetizers and such. So, I was thinking, should we pray over our dessert since this is our main meal?" Lucy laughed, "Well, what is the answer?" Joseph joked, "We would have prayed over the main meal so let's call this our main meal and say a prayer." Lucy replied, "Awesome! Shall we then?" She reached over to hold Joseph's hand, "Thank you, Lord, for putting Joseph in my path again. Bless this dessert. I know Jesus has a sweet tooth. Therefore, Jesus, please join us for dessert. May we not gain any pounds from all these calories?" Joseph laughed, "Let's dig in!"

Joseph asked, "So you were saying that your mom got you late in life. How old was she?" Lucy smiled as she took the first bite of her German Chocolate Cake. "Oh my, this is delicious! Would you like to try it?" Joseph smiled, "Sure!" Lucy answered Joseph's question, "Mom and dad got married in their thirties. Busy yuppies, you know. Anyway, when mom finally decided she wanted a family, she had trouble getting pregnant. After quite a few years, they finally decided to adopt and found me. She was forty-five. Daddy was ten years older than she was. That may have been part of the problem. I do not know." Joseph laughed, "I can tell you; it was God's plan." Lucy smiled at him, "You think so?" Joseph replied, "Absolutely. I am very confident about that. So that makes your mom around seventyish?" Lucy looked surprised, "Yes. How did you know that?" Joseph laughed, "I just figured you were about my age." Lucy asked with a grin, "What is your age?" Joseph laughed, "I am 26." Lucy laughed, "Well, I am a year younger than you." Joseph smiled, "I thought so. You must try my Coconut Cake." Lucy smiled, "I thought you would never invite me to taste it." She reached over and took a bite and smiled, "Wow! The cake is delicious! I wish I could bake like this."

Joseph asked, "Have you tried?" Lucy shyly replied, "I have to say, I am not very good in the kitchen. I started flying shortly after high school." Joseph asked, "You said your parents were yuppies, so what did they do?" Lucy replied, "My dad was a doctor and worked 24/7. I don't remember him being around much." Joseph replied, "I am sorry you did not see him much." Lucy smiled, "It is okay. Mom was a lawyer, so she too was very busy; I grew up with a nanny." Joseph asked, "How did she affect your life?" Lucy asked, "What do you mean?" Joseph

asked, "Was she nice to you?" Lucy replied, "Well, I had a few."
Joseph asked, "A few?"

Lucy answered, "Yeah from when I was born until five, Rosa was my
nanny. She loved me; I learned what love was from her. Rosa had to
go back to Mexico to care for her family; I cried for months when she
left. I was not nice to my next nanny. I guess I had hoped that Rosa
would come back. Nancy left after a year and told my mom that I was
out of control. She could not handle me. Next, Olga came into my life
and was extremely strict with me. She was militant and very cold-
hearted. It was her way or no way. My mom tolerated her for a few
years, then decided I needed someone to be more of a friend.
Therefore, at the age of nine, Karen came into my life. Karen was so
sweet and yet young enough to understand me! She was originally
from Guatemala but spoke perfect English. Karen was a college
student studying Sociology. The arrangement worked out great for
mom because I was in school, so she did not need to have someone at
the house all day. Karen earned one weekend off a month. She did
the entire school drop-off and picked up, helped me with homework,
and made my meals. Karen and I became excellent friends. She
returned to Guatemala when I entered high school."

Joseph smiled, "Are you still friends?" Lucy smiled, "Yes, we are still
good friends. We are always in touch. She moved back to Guatemala
and is making a difference in her country." Joseph asked, "When was
the last time you saw her?" Lucy smiled, "I see her at least once a
year. I started traveling so I could go see her." Joseph asked, "How did
you get started?" Lucy replied, "My father had a patient that was a
pilot, and he was the one that helped me get started in this career."
Joseph replied, "Wow! It helps to know people. Why weren't you
interested in your parents' careers?" Lucy smiled, "I did not want to
miss out on my family as they did. I knew one day I would get married
and have a family. I want to be a real mom." Joseph replied, "That
makes perfect sense."

Lucy asked, "What about you?" Joseph thought for a moment, "I want
to be a good daddy when it's time. I lost my mom when I was very
young. I was seven. I then lost my mean, alcoholic dad in high school.

I have been alone since mom went to heaven." Lucy replied, "I am so sorry for your loss." She reached over and gently touched his hand. Joseph lifted his eyes and smiled at her, "I am okay. When Papa came into my life, everything changed for me." Lucy smiled, "I know. However, I perceived that you had never heard anyone say that they were truly sorry for your loss." Joseph thought for a moment, "You know, you are right. I did not hear those words as a kid. Maybe my uncle, but I cannot remember. Also, I may have just been in shock and not heard it." Lucy smiled at him. Joseph added, "Thank you, Lucy."

Lucy asked, "Have you ever thought about what your future wife will be like?" Joseph laughed, "Well, I guess I should have asked Joey? He knew what his new dad would look like, the whole works." Lucy laughed, "He did seem to have things figured out. He sure was a cute little boy." Joseph added, "I thought it was cute that he kept saying that I was him in the future."

Suddenly Joseph's phone rang, "Excuse me. I should take this call. Hello? Joseph speaking." He smiled as he heard Joey's voice, 'Joseph can you see me tomorrow?' Joseph responded, "Hello, Joey. Yes, of course, I can come. Can you have your mom text me your address? Did you make it home?" Joey answered, 'No, but I told mommy I want you to see me. She said it was okay.' Joseph asked, "What time should I come?" Joey giggled, 'Can you come when you wake up?' Joseph laughed, "How about I come for lunch? I can take you and your mommy out to eat." Joey screamed with joy, 'Yes! I love to go out to eat!' Joseph was laughing, "Okay. Think about where you want to go, and I will drive us there." Joey handed the phone to his mommy, 'I am sorry this is short notice. Joey was insisting that you would come.' Joseph smiled, "It is my pleasure. I do not have any plans for a couple of days, so I am happy to come by. Please text your address to me, and I will be there at 11:30." Sophia responded, 'Thank you for being so kind to my Joey. He loves you.' Joseph replied, "I love him too. It is Godly love. I will not let him down. We can talk tomorrow." Sophia handed Joey the phone, 'Bye, Joseph. See you tomorrow.'

Lucy smiled, "You make such an impact on people that they will become your extended family. That little boy loves you. Don't be surprised if he asks you to be his daddy." Joseph laughed, "I don't look like the daddy he is looking for."

Joseph changed the subject, "When did you find out that you were adopted?" Lucy laughed, "Changing the subject? I don't look like either one of my parents, so it was something they lovingly broke to me when I was old enough to understand. I was tiny when my mom told me that I was a special gift the stork brought." Joseph asked, "What? A stork?" Lucy added, "I think it was her way of opening up the conversation." Joseph asked, "Did you ever want to meet your birth parents?" Lucy smiled, "I did for a while but never tried. It was not a priority for me. I have family, so I thought I didn't need more." Joseph thought, "I wonder if I am setting myself up for disappointment?" Lucy asked, "Why would you think that?" Joseph added, "I hadn't thought about what my mother would feel." Lucy smiled at him, "Listen, you are such a wonderful man, your mother will be happy to meet you finally, and besides, God is leading you. Don't doubt that." Joseph smiled, "Thanks. You are right; I would not have met Ahanu if it was not God's will."

Lucy looked at her plate, "How did I finish all this dessert?" Joseph laughed, "I did help you; you know. You did not eat all those calories." Lucy was laughing, "Talking and eating is a very bad combination. I didn't even realize all the cake was gone." Joseph teased, "I thought you were getting ready to lick the plate." Lucy picked up her plate, "Oh, I will!" Joseph laughed as she licked her plate. "Lucy, you crack me up! I hope you do not eat like this all the time." Lucy was giggling, "I can if I want to!"

Joseph smiled at Lucy, "I hate to break up our fun, but I need to get my car rental." Lucy smiled, "I know. I was fretting this moment. I have enjoyed my time with you." Joseph smiled, "I have enjoyed this time as well. Let's meet up again." Lucy responded, "I would love that. Let me know when you are available, and we can connect." Joseph smiled, "I don't know what my schedule will be, but I do have lunch with Joey tomorrow." Lucy laughed, "Yeah, he got dibs on you first." Joseph laughed, "He sure did!"

Joseph gathered his luggage and handed Lucy hers. Lucy came around the table and hugged him, and softly whispered, "You are a beautiful creation from God. You bless everyone you meet and carry peace and hope. Thank you for your obedience." Joseph wrapped his arms around Lucy and replied, "Thank you for your kind words. Continue to allow Yah to speak through you. I needed to hear those words today."

Lucy reached down to pick up her luggage. She wiped tears away. "Joseph, I can honestly say that I feel like I have known you all my life." Joseph replied, "It's incredible how the Lord works. The people I meet have become my extended family. At a time when I had no one, He has brought so many wonderful people into my life."

Joseph picked up his luggage. "Once I see Ahanu, I will call you to set up another meetup." Lucy responded, "That sounds like a plan! Talk to you soon!" Joseph asked, "How are you getting home?" Lucy answered, "I normally take a shuttle. It will take me all the way home." Joseph asked, "May I give you a ride home?" Lucy laughed, "Are you sure? I don't want you to go out of your way." Joseph replied, "I would not have asked if it would be an inconvenience." Lucy smiled, "Well then, I will take a ride!"

Joseph asked, "Is your mother expecting you for dinner?" Lucy asked, "No, why?" Joseph was grinning, "Why don't you join me for dinner. I know Ahanu and his family would love to meet you." Lucy asked, "Are you sure?" Joseph laughed, "Of course I am. I will just let Ahanu know we have one more for dinner." Lucy asked, "Are you sure they don't mind?" Joseph replied, "I am sure! Ahanu knows me. I am very unpredictable." Lucy laughed, "Okay. Let him know but give him the option to say no." Joseph laughed, "You will get used to me. I am obedient to Yah only."

Joseph walked in as they reached his car rental hub and smiled, "Hello. I have a car." The young man at the counter smiled, "Yes, you do. You must be Mr. Arias. May I call you Joseph?" Joseph was a little surprised because he hadn't given his name yet. He asked, "How did you know?" He laughed, "You wouldn't believe me if I told you." Joseph said, "Try me." The young man continued, "Okay. Let me tell you, it is weird. I dreamt of you last night. Jesus Christ told me to give you the best car because you were here on a special ops mission. I admit that I did not believe in Jesus until I awoke. I knew I would see you today." Joseph laughed, "Yeah, that's my King! Papa is in charge of my life." Joseph looked at the young man's nametag, "Eric, you said you didn't believe. What did you believe?" Eric replied, "I grew up with atheist parents, so I never heard about God or Jesus. When I awoke, I prayed for the first time in my life. I told Jesus, if you are real, I want to see this Joseph guy. And now, you walk in."

Lucy began to laugh in the back. Joseph turned to her, "What's so funny?" She replied, "God continues to impress me." Eric added, "I only saw Joseph; I did not see you." Lucy, still laughing added, "I am a last-minute addition." Joseph smiled, "It's a long story. Eric, I am glad you are now a believer in Christ Jesus. So what car am I supposed to get?" Eric replied, "In my dream, Jesus told me to show you favor. I will give you free upgrades. I reserved a blue Porsche Cayenne." Joseph smiled, "Thank you, Eric, for being obedient. Thank you, Yah, for this blessing." Eric asked, "Are you able to say what your mission is?" Joseph laughed, "I am not sure. I don't always know until I arrive or set foot where I am going." Eric responded, "I see. I hope I see you when you return the car." Joseph smiled, "I hope so too."

Joseph asked Eric, "May I pray for you?" Eric smiled, "Sure! I have never had anyone pray for me." Joseph began, "Abba Father, thank you for Eric. Bless him in everything that he does. Open his eyes and ears, give him discernment to know when it is You speaking to him. I ask this in the Name of Your Beloved, Mighty Son, Christ Jesus. Amen." Eric smiled, "Thank you. I feel different. Don't know how to explain it." Joseph responded, "Get ready to have fun with God."

Joseph and Lucy headed out to the car. Joseph asked, "Do you know how to get to Golden?" Lucy replied, "Yes, I do. My mom lives in Golden, and I live in Wheat Ridge, not far from Golden." Joseph replied, "See, it is not out of my way." Lucy laughed, "It is all in God's plan." Joseph was glad to see that the car had a navigation system. He set the address, and off they traveled.

Lucy asked, "So what did Ahanu and his family say when you said you had one more?" Joseph laughed, "He said the more, the merrier. We have a house full." Lucy suddenly felt self-conscience, "If they have a family to greet you, I don't want to intrude." Joseph smiled, "Don't worry about it. You are my family too." Lucy felt a little better, "Okay. I guess I better get used to this." Joseph added, "Yeah, you better. You will have more family tonight than you know what to do with. Ahanu and his wife are very welcoming. They felt right at home in my home."

Lucy decided to change the subject. She asked, "So tell me what you know about your mother." Joseph replied, "Well, honestly, I don't know much. YAH showed her to me in a dream. I saw her face when she was about 14 or 15 years old. She was alone and giving birth to me." Lucy softly responded, "Oh my. I see. Do you hope to find her at this reunion?" Joseph replied, "If it is Yah's will. I will meet her this weekend. Ahanu believes that she must be family. Why else would we look so much alike?"

Lucy carefully asked, "Have you thought about what you would ask her?" Joseph smiled, "Yes, I have." Lucy asked, "And?" Joseph sighed, "First, I would introduce myself. Ask her name. Then ask if she knows the Creator. Then explain that I dreamt of her. I pray one thing would lead to another, and I could say you are my mother." Lucy asked, "What if she denies being your mother?" Joseph frowned, "I pray she doesn't. However, if she did, I would say sorry. I must have confused you with someone else. And ask for her forgiveness." Lucy reached over, grabbed his hand, and squeezed it. She said, "I pray she, too, has been looking for you. I want a happy ending for you."

Joseph laughed, "It will be a happy ending either way. If she denies having me, she doesn't deserve me. I can then end this quest. But, on the other hand if she accepts me, I will have my mother again. What more do I need? I have YHVH!" Lucy smiled, "I will be interceding for you the entire weekend. I will text you if I see something or hear something."

They pulled up to Ahanu's house. Something felt very familiar to Joseph. Joseph said, "I feel like I have been here before." Lucy asked, "This is the first time in Denver, right?" Joseph replied, "Well, I think so. I grew up in Nebraska, not too far from here."

Joseph saw Ahanu come running out of the house screaming. Ahanu yelled, "What took you so long!" Joseph laughed, "It is so good to see you again. Let me introduce you to Lucy." Ahanu gathered himself, "I am Ahanu. Joseph's brother from another mother." Lucy laughed, "Oh my goodness. You do look so much alike." Ahanu asked, "Which of us is better looking?" Lucy laughed, "Well, you are, of course!" Ahanu said, "I love you already! Come on in, please. We can get your luggage later."

As they entered the front door, Meekaila ran to Joseph and jumped into his arms, "Uncle, I am so happy to see you!" Joseph was laughing, "I am super happy to see you too. Let me introduce you to my friend Lucy. Lucy, this is Meekaila." Lucy reached out to shake her hand, but Meekaila threw her arms around Lucy. Meekaila said, "Lucy. I love that name! I have a doll named Lucy." As Meekaila hugged both Joseph and Lucy, Ahanu pulled her away. Ahanu said, "You can't hog them all to yourself. We must introduce them to the family." Meekaila made a pouty face, "But he's my uncle first." Joseph smiled, "I will always be your uncle first." Meekaila smiled and grabbed Lucy's hand. She led her to the backyard, and Joseph and Ahanu followed.

Ahanu got everyone's attention, "Hey everyone. Let me introduce you to Joseph, my twin, and his friend Lucy." Ahanu smiled, "I will allow everyone to introduce themselves to you. It will be easier than going around and naming them. Would you like tea, lemonade, or soda?" Joseph answered, "Lemonade, please." Lucy said, "Make that two." Ahanu disappeared into the crowd.

Meekaila was doing all the introductions. Then she led them to the table and sat between them. Everyone started to grab a seat. Joseph smiled at Lucy, "Are you doing, okay?" Lucy shook her head, "Yes, I am. I have my new young friend to show me around." Isabella and a few women started to bring out the dishes full of food. The aromas coming from the food were delicious and inviting. As they placed each platter down, Joseph smiled. Joseph whispered to Lucy, "Now this is home-cooked comfort food." Lucy answered, "I have never seen this much food on a table." Meekaila giggled, "This is how we eat every weekend."

When the ladies had finished placing the platters on the table, Ahanu spoke, "Today is a special day. You all get to meet Joseph and welcome him to our family reunion. Joseph, would you do the honor of thanking God for this meal?" Joseph replied, "I would be honored. Thank you, Creator, for everyone here today. Thank you for the abundance. Bless the hands that prepared this delicious meal. Thank you for Your Son, Jesus Christ. Father, Son, and Holy Spirit, please join us today. Amen."

Joseph asked, "Who were the cooks of this delicious meal?" Meekaila said, "Mommy and daddy cooked most of it, but my uncles and aunts also brought some food." Joseph replied, "So it was a whole family cook-off. That's awesome." Lucy added, "The food looks delicious. Thank you for having us." Joseph looked at his plate and shook his head, "I don't know how I will eat all of this, but I will." Meekaila laughed, "My daddy can eat two huge plates like that." Ahanu laughed, "Meekaila, don't give away all my secrets."

Lucy smiled at all the conversation that was happening all at once. She couldn't keep up, so she tried to focus on a couple of people asking Joseph questions. Lucy wasn't sure how Joseph was able to keep up with everyone. But she knew he felt right at home. Lucy smiled at Meekaila, "How do you keep up with everyone?" Meekaila giggled, "Uncle Pete is always talking about bears because he loves to hunt. Uncle Romie is always talking about eating healthy; you can tell he works out. Aunt Genie is always talking about her kids. She is always busy taking them to sports and dance. Great aunt Pauline is always talking about her dogs, all five. Great uncle Mike talks about cars because he is a mechanic and can fix any car. The cousins are always talking about school. Some are in college, some are in high school, and a lot are in grade school. Uncle Jay is too busy on his phone to talk. I think it is his girlfriend, who is very pretty. She didn't want to come today. Grandpa and grandma are always talking to all the kids. They like to make them laugh. Grandpa sometimes makes jokes." Lucy smiled, "How about you? What do you like to talk about?" Meekaila laughed, "I like to talk about everything. While we waited for you, I told them how Uncle Joseph taught me to surf. That was so much fun." Lucy laughed, "I see. So, you were the entertainment while you waited." Meekaila laughed, "I am always."

After dinner, Isabella brought out some cake and ice cream. Joseph laughed, "Oh yeah! Bring on the cake!" Joseph and Lucy looked at each other and giggled. Lucy said, "I am so full, but I can always make room for cake." Meekaila laughed, "Me too."

As the evening was winding down, Lucy smiled at Joseph, "I can take a cab home. I don't want to pull you away from your family." Meekaila heard her and responded, "You can stay in my room, Lucy." Lucy smiled, "I have a house not too far from here. I should sleep in my bed. But thank you for the offer." Joseph replied, "Meekaila and I can take you home. It is not a problem." Meekaila ran to Ahanu, "Can I go with Uncle Joseph and take Lucy home?" Ahanu answered, "Why don't we both go. I will drive because Meekaila has her car seat."

The drive to Lucy's was quick and fun. They laughed the entire way. Finally, Ahanu said, "Lucy, you are now family so expect to get invited to come over every weekend." Lucy replied, "Thank you. I would love to come. But unfortunately, I fly out of town a lot, so I may not always be home." Ahanu replied, "You can come when you're home."

Lucy got out of the car and said her goodbyes. Joseph exited the vehicle, "I will walk you to the house and ensure everything is safe." As Lucy unlocked the house, she turned off the alarm and said, "Thanks for being my friend. Text me and let me know when we can meet again. Joseph replied, "I will. I feel you will be over to the house many times before I leave." Lucy laughed, "I hope so. I enjoyed myself today." Joseph responded, "Well, good night. May you have prophetic dreams. Talk to you tomorrow."

Lucy closed the door, and Joseph walked back to the car. As he got into the passenger seat, Meekaila asked, "Is Lucy your girlfriend?" Joseph laughed, "No. She is just a new friend." Ahanu laughed, "I can see how sweet she is on you. She feels right at home with you." Joseph shook his head, "I think most people feel at home with me because Creator put them in my life." Ahanu continued to tease him, "Sure. Whatever you say. I see the chemistry. Meekaila, what do you see?" Meekaila was giggling, "Uncle Joseph, she looks at you like you are her prince. Didn't you see her all night long?" Joseph replied with a chuckle, "Okay, you two. I just met her recently. Today is only the second time I have seen her." Meekaila continued to giggle, "You should have kissed her good night. My daddy always kisses me good night." Joseph laughed, "Meekaila, that's different. I am not her daddy."

Ahanu decided to change the subject. He asked, "So tell me. How did you meet?" Joseph laughed, "She was the flight attendant on my flight back from Europe. Surprisingly, she was my flight attendant flying here. She had just changed from international to domestic flights to be closer to her mom." Ahanu asked, "That must be Creator, right?" Joseph smiled, "Yeah, I do think it's Yah." Ahanu asked, "When do you want to settle down? Have a wife and family." Joseph laughed, "I don't know. I have much work to do for the Creator. That comes first." Ahanu laughed, "What if He is saying that now is the right timing?" Joseph laughed, "Can we drop this?" Ahanu pressed, "Just answer the question." Meekaila also teased, "Uncle Joey, just answer the question." Joseph was laughing, "Okay. If it is time, the first thing I need to do is make sure I am over my high school sweetheart. I would have to find her and talk to her. She was my best friend. If that is over, then I can look somewhere else."

Ahanu teased, "Oh, the plot thickens. Who is your first love? Where does she live?" Joseph smiled, "Honestly, I don't know." Meekaila asked, "How did you lose her?" Joseph laughed, "I lost her a long time ago when I went to college. I broke her heart." Meekaila was sad, "I am so sorry, Uncle Joey. I did not mean to make you sad." Joseph smiled, "I am not sad. It's okay. I need to get through this weekend. Then I can think about other things."

Meekaila asked, "Can we have more cake when we get home?" Joseph laughed, "Now, that's a good question!" Ahanu smiled, "Honey, it is pretty late. Not sure mommy would want you to get a tummy ache." Meekaila made a pouty face, "I won't get a tummy ache. I can have some ice cream because it always makes my tummy feel better." Joseph laughed, "That must run in the family. My tummy always feels better when I have ice cream." Ahanu replied, "Joseph, you are not helping me." Joseph laughed, "What if it is a tiny piece?" Meekaila cheered, "Yes! A tiny piece, daddy." Ahanu laughed, "Okay, but it is just this once because your uncle is here." Joseph and Meekaila cheered, "Yay!"

Upon their return, people were starting to leave. Joseph thanked everyone for their hospitality. Then he and Meekaila made a beeline to the cake. Isabella caught them, "What do you think you are doing?" Meekaila laughed, "Uncle Joey wanted cake, mommy. I can't let him eat alone." Isabella laughed, "Well, if you have cake, I better get the ice cream out." Joseph laughed, "I hope it's okay." Isabella answered, "Actually, I also wanted another slice of cake." Ahanu laughed, "So that's where Meekaila gets it from." Joseph asked, "Ahanu, can I serve you a slice? We do not want to make you feel left out."

They laughed for the rest of the night. They shared stories of the winters in the cold country. It was almost midnight when they headed to bed. It would be a busy weekend.

Chapter 20 Amitola

Joseph awoke early. It was five am. He was excited and felt like a small child anticipating opening a gift. He went through his routine. 'Thank you, Yah, for a great night's rest. Today I ask for and receive an abundance of grace. I am here and ready to receive any messages or words You need me to speak. I am willing to do as You ask. Thank You, Yah, for Your love. Thank You for your guidance.' Joseph got up, put on his running clothes, headed out the back door and out of the backyard. He took a deep breath and smiled. 'Which way, Yah?' He heard, 'Go left.' Joseph chuckled, 'Yes, YAH.'

Joseph had been running for a few minutes when he noticed a woman walking toward a car. He kept his eye on her. Suddenly, the woman slipped and fell. He ran to her and offered help. Joseph asked, "I saw you fall. May I help you up?" The woman looked up at him, "Yes, please." He reached down and took her hand. She took hold of his arm. He lifted her and asked, "Are you okay?" She replied, "I think I am okay. I don't feel any pain. Thank you for your help." Joseph watched her closely, "Can you stand on your own?" She replied, "Maybe. I am feeling very dizzy. Can you help me to the door? My husband is inside." Joseph continued to support her, "Is he awake?" She looked at Joseph with some concern, "Yes. He may be in the kitchen." Joseph decided he should introduce himself, "My name is Joseph." She looked at him, "I am Amitola. My husband is Harvey." As they opened the door, she called out to her husband, "Harvey. I need your help." Harvey came running, "What's the matter?" Amitola answered, "I fell. I don't know what happened. This young man happened to be jogging by and helped me up." Joseph smiled, "Hello, my name is Joseph. I saw Amitola slip. It appeared that she might have hit her head."

Harvey decided that he needed to call 911. Joseph asked, "Amitola, may I pray for you?" Amitola shook her head, "I am okay. I feel sleepy." Joseph asked again, "May I say a prayer for you?" She did not reply. He began to pray, "Lord, I ask that You send your Heavenly Healing Host to heal Amitola. Fight this battle for her. There will be no permanent damage due to this fall. I speak healing in Jesus' name." Joseph continued to engage in conversation with Amitola, but she kept falling asleep. Joseph decided to wait until the ambulance arrived. Finally, Amitola opened her eyes to say, "Thank you for your kindness and help." Harvey eventually joined them, "Thank God you came along when you did. Thank you for helping my wife." Finally, they heard the ambulance; it felt like an eternity. Harvey ran outside to wave them down. As the paramedics worked on Amitola, Joseph thanked Yah, "Yah, thank you for bringing me in this direction. Heavenly hosts surround the ambulance. Yah guide the hands of the medics and doctors."

Joseph decided he should head back and jogged back to Ahanu's house. He wondered why Amitola had slipped; there was no ice or anything on the driveway to make her trip. Joseph couldn't shake the feeling that he knew Amitola. As he struggled to make sense of her fall, he also attempted to remember her face. He thought to himself, 'This is weird; I cannot remember her face.' He struggled to remember, then he asked, 'Yah, why can't I remember Amitola's face? I am normally good at remembering faces. I do not understand why I can't even remember her eyes.' Silence. He did not hear a reply from Yah. He thought this was very weird, and he asked again, 'Yah? Are you there? Why can't I remember Amitola?' Silence. All Joseph could hear were his footsteps. Joseph stopped. He looked around. 'I know I always hear you. Why can't I hear you now?' Suddenly, he heard an audible voice, "I am here." Joseph smiled, "Yah, I was afraid you had left me." He heard a chuckle, "You know I never leave you." Joseph asked again, "Yah, why can't I remember her face?" Yah answered, "You do." Joseph closed his eyes, and he remembered Harvey.

Harvey was a handsome man. He looked like he was in his 50's. Although his eyes were gentle, he seemed very worried about his wife.

Amitola's face was coming into focus. She was quite beautiful, her face was a beautiful tan color, and she had kind eyes. He could tell that she was a very kind, loving person. Suddenly he remembered the look on her face. She looked surprised. Joseph had smiled at her and had reassured her that she would be all right. 'Thank You, Yah.'

As he arrived at Ahanu's house, he felt exhausted. He entered the backyard and back door. He snuck into the house unseen and headed back to the bedroom. He slipped off his shoes and fell to his knees as he entered the room. He crawled across the room. He didn't understand what was happening to him. Finally, he reached the bed and slipped under the covers. His eyes were extremely heavy, and he fell asleep.

Joseph awoke to a knock on the door. Ahanu opened the door and popped his head in, "Are you awake?" Joseph replied, "I am now. What time is it?" Ahanu answered, "It's nine. Are you okay?" Joseph replied, "I think so. I had the strangest experience this morning." Ahanu had entered the room, "Oh yeah. What's going on?"

Joseph smiled, "Well, I went out for a run but didn't get very far." Ahanu asked, "What happened?" Joseph continued, "As I ran, I saw a woman. She was out on her driveway, getting into her car. I saw her fall and hit her head." Ahanu reacted, "What? Oh my!" Joseph continued, "I helped her into her house. Her husband Harvey was home and called the ambulance." Ahanu continued to ask questions, "Is she okay? Who was she?" Joseph continued, "Her name is Amitola. I am sure she's okay. I prayed for her before the paramedics arrived." Ahanu replied, "You did have a busy morning. Are you okay?" Joseph responded, "I am fine, but I do not understand why I am not getting clarity. I returned, and I was so sleepy by the time I arrived. Almost didn't make it into bed." Ahanu asked, "How do you feel now?" Joseph answered, "I feel fine. I remember the look she had on her face when she saw me. She looked surprised." Ahanu laughed and joked, "You know it is because you are so good-looking!" Joseph smiled, "Yeah, I am sure that was it. Do you know her?" Ahanu replied, "I can't remember meeting neighbors named Harvey and

Amitola. Amitola, I would remember that name." Joseph asked, "Why is that?" Ahanu smirked, "Have you ever heard that name?" Joseph replied, "No, but that doesn't mean anything." Ahanu smiled, "That is a Native American name." Joseph laughed, "Oh, I see. Before you tell me anything else, let me say that I saw a rainbow above her head." Ahanu shook his head, "You see, Yah showed you what her name means. Amitola means rainbow."

Joseph thought, "It doesn't only mean rainbow, but it means promise. The rainbow is the sign Yah gave us promising not to destroy the earth by flood again."

Ahanu said, "What if she is connected to your promise? You always say nothing is a coincidence." Joseph replied, "I felt like I knew her. However, I have never seen her before. The other strange thing is the feeling I had of exhaustion once I arrived back here. What do you think that could be?" Ahanu reasoned, "You did have a long flight, and maybe you haven't rested enough. You also just finished a huge job." Joseph was in deep thought, "Maybe." Ahanu pressed, "What are you thinking?" Joseph responded, "Well, I can't shake the feeling of knowing her. It just seems different. When I meet someone that I have dreamt it is a different feeling of knowing them." Ahanu replied, "Maybe it is the prayer you said for her that took all you had? Last night was a big emotional deal too." Joseph answered, "Now that is a possibility. Okay, so what's on for today's agenda?" Ahanu replied, "Well, let's have breakfast and see what the ladies have planned."

Joseph jumped out of bed and asked, "Do I have time for a quick shower?" Ahanu teased, "I was hoping you wouldn't come out smelling like this. The girls may faint." Joseph laughed and headed to the shower.

After his shower, Joseph entered the kitchen. "Something sure smells delicious. Meekaila, are you the chef?" Meekaila ran to Joseph, "Good morning, Uncle Joey, you woke up." Joseph replied, "Yeah, your daddy woke me up. I guess I was exhausted today." Meekaila giggled, "I heard you get up early in the morning. Where did you go?" Joseph smiled at her, "I went for a jog but was too tired, so I went back to sleep." Joseph turned to Isabella, "Good morning, Isabella. How are you today?" Isabella smiled, "Good morning. It is a beautiful day. I prepared a little dish we like to have after a night of overeating."

Joseph asked, "What is it?" Meekaila giggled, "It is called menudo. I am going to have oatmeal. Do you want some oatmeal?" Joseph smiled, "I have never had menudo. I think I will try that." Meekaila laughed, "I will make you a bowl of oatmeal too." Joseph replied, "Okay. That sounds good."

Isabella placed a bowl in front of Joseph, "Joseph, you are welcome to add any of these condiments to your liking." Joseph saw raw chopped onions, oregano, cilantro, lemon, and lime wedges, and crushed red peppers. Joseph laughed, "I am not going to ask what this is made from but from Meekaila's reaction, she does not like it." Meekaila was plugging her nose. Ahanu laughed, "She is a little picky. I am sure that you will like it. If not, Meekaila has oatmeal ready for you." Meekaila added, "I know you will not like it, Uncle. You might as well eat oatmeal." Joseph laughed, "Meekaila, you are scaring me." Joseph took a sip of the broth. "I like the broth, and it is quite tasty. Ahanu, what do you like to add?" Ahanu replied, "I add everything."

Joseph started putting in a little of everything then sampled the broth again; "It does taste good. Meekaila, why don't you like this?" Meekaila took a bite of oatmeal, "The menudo is squishy. I do not like anything squishy." Joseph had just tasted the menudo, "Oh, I see." He said as he swallowed his bite. He said to Meekaila, "I see what you mean." Joseph ate some of the hominy and smiled, "This is tasty. I can do without the squishy stuff, though." Meekaila was giggling, "Are you ready for your oatmeal?" Joseph laughed, "I can eat this. I do like it." Ahanu laughed, "You don't have to eat this." Joseph laughed, "No. I like the hominy, broth, and condiments." Isabella laughed, "The face you made was priceless and very telling of your reaction to the tripe." Joseph asked, "What is tripe?"

Meekaila replied, "Uncle Joey, you do not want to know." Joseph laughed, "Oh, come on. I think I do." Ahanu joined in, "No, you don't want to know." Isabella laughed, "Oh, it's not that bad. I grew up eating this stuff." Joseph's interest was being peaked, "Now, I think I need to know." Isabella replied, "Tripe comes from either the first or second cow's stomach." Joseph began to laugh, "Is this nutritious?" Isabella replied, "It is very nutritious. It is high in protein, packed with vitamins A, B12, and folate. It is low fat. It is also a good source of other minerals." Joseph smiled, "Isabella, I had no idea. I believe I had heard of menudo but never had any. I also never looked for it at a restaurant."

Meekaila asked, "Are you going to eat it because it's healthy?" Joseph laughed, "No way! I am a texture person, and I can't." Joseph smiled at Isabella, "Sorry, Isabella. I like the broth and hominy but can't take another bite of the tripe." Isabella smiled, "It's okay. It is an acquired taste. At least you can now say that you have experienced menudo." Joseph laughed, "Yes, I have. Thank you for expanding my culinary experience." Meekaila teased, "Now, are you ready for your oatmeal?" Joseph replied, "I will eat that after finishing my bowl of menudo without the tripe."

Meekaila asked, "Are we going out for lunch today?" Joseph suddenly remembered, "Oh no. I almost forgot that I made a lunch date with a boy named Joey and his mom. Joey sat with me on the flight here. His mother reached out yesterday before I left the airport to request a lunch date. Meekaila, maybe you could come along and meet Joey. I think you would get along very well. He does not have many friends." Meekaila asked her parents, "Mommy and daddy can I go, please?" Isabella asked, "Would it be okay if we all came along?" Joseph replied, "Of course it is! I think it would be great for them to meet you. I will text them and tell them that we will all meet up with them."

Joseph sent a text. 'Hello, Sophia and Joey. My friend and his family would appreciate it if they could join us. I hope it's okay that I invited them. Let me know if you prefer not to have us all. Meekaila is seven years old.' Joseph said, "May this be Your will, Yah." He sent the text and waited. The response was quick. 'We would love to meet all your friends. Is Lucy coming too?' Joseph chuckled, "I will see if she would be available.' Joseph sent a text to Lucy. 'Good morning, Lucy! Would you be able to join us to meet up with Joey and his mom?' Lucy replied immediately, 'I would love to! Can my mom come too?'

Joseph chuckled and said to Ahanu, "The number increases as the minutes go by." Joseph replied to Lucy, 'The more, the merrier!' Joseph texted Sophia, 'Lucy and her mom will join us too. Where shall we meet?' Sophia responded, 'We can come to you if that's okay?' Joseph asked Ahanu, "Is it okay if everyone comes here?" Ahanu replied, "That would be awesome!" Joseph replied to Sophia and Lucy, 'my friend Ahanu says, please come on over.' Joseph sent the address.

Joseph put his phone down, "Okay. Let's get to work. What shall we have for lunch?" Ahanu asked, "What do you feel like?" Joseph smiled, "You know me, I love BBQs." Meekaila cheered, "Yay! I want hotdogs and hamburgers." Joseph replied, "That sounds good to me." Isabella added, "Okay, let's get some potatoes, and I will make a potato salad. What do we want for dessert?" Ahanu asked, "Do we still have some pecan pie?" Isabella answered, "Yes, we do. They are in the garage fridge." Joseph laughed, "Ahanu and Isabella, I'm impressed with your preparation for unexpected company." Ahanu replied, "We usually have family over quite often, so we are always prepared. We need to run out to get buns." Joseph said, "Let's go. Where is the nearest grocery store?"

Suddenly his phone beeped. Lucy had sent a text. He read the text aloud, "What can we bring?" Ahanu smiled, "If she wants to bring chips, otherwise, we can grab them. Joseph replied, 'Chips or whatever you'd like.' Lucy replied, 'Do you not trust my cooking?' Joseph laughed, 'That's exactly why I said whatever you like.' Lucy replied, "I will bring my world-famous mac and cheese. Meekaila and Joey will love it.' Joseph replied, 'That sounds like a great thing to add to the BBQ.' Joseph announced, "Lucy is bringing Mac and Cheese." Meekaila cheered, "Yummy!"

Ahanu spoke to Isabella, "We are going to the grocery store. Let me know if you need anything else. Come on, Joseph." Joseph asked, "Isabella, do you want help with the potatoes before leaving?" Isabella answered, "No. I am good. Meekaila will help me. You boys have fun." Joseph grabbed his keys, "I'm driving." Ahanu replied, "I was hoping to take a ride in your fancy car."

Joseph shared the story of the car. "I arrived at my car rental, and Eric greeted me by name. He had a dream where Jesus told him to show me favor. So, he reserved this car for me and gave me huge discounts. He said that he had grown up with atheist parents and never knew about Jesus." Ahanu responded, "That is amazing. What a cool story he has to share."

The men went into the grocery store, and Joseph grabbed a cart. They talked about the family reunion as they found the things they needed. Joseph asked, "When do we go to the family reunion?" Ahanu apologized, "Sorry I hadn't given you details. We head out at 9 am, and we are about an hour away. This year we had it catered, so we don't have to worry about bringing food. We go and party." Joseph added, "I would be happy to pay for my meal." Ahanu smiled, "I know you would. You are my guest, so don't worry about a thing. Besides, we have some wealthy family members that have paid for everything." Joseph replied, "Okay, I won't worry about anything." Ahanu asked, "Do you think Lucy would like to come? She would fit right in." Joseph smiled, "I don't know, but she will be here soon, so you can ask her."

As they got into the car, Joseph asked, "Would you be okay if we stopped and checked to see if Amitola is home?" Ahanu answered, "Of course. This way, I too can meet my neighbor." Joseph smiled, "Do you ever have a neighborhood party?" Ahanu replied, "We sometimes do it during the summer, but we haven't organized it for a few years. Isabella has been so busy with work." Joseph smiled, "I haven't been to a block party since I was young. I think my mom was still alive." Ahanu added, "The reunion will be like a block party. I know you will enjoy yourself."

As they approached Amitola's house, Joseph glanced over at Ahanu. Ahanu was looking at something. Joseph asked, "What do you see?" Ahanu glanced at Joseph, "Do you see the rainbow?" Joseph answered, "Yes. I wondered if it was visible to you too." Ahanu said, "I have not seen such a bright rainbow. The colors look alive." Joseph parked in front of the house. Joseph asked, "Are you coming in with me?" Ahanu was still looking at the rainbow, "I will try to record this. Go ahead. I will come in a second."

Joseph walked to the door and rang the doorbell. He waited — no answer. So, he rang the doorbell again. He finally heard a voice, "Just a minute." Harvey answered the door, and Joseph reintroduced himself, "Hello, I'm Joseph. I saw your wife fall. I just wanted to check on her." Harvey opened the door wider, "I am glad you found her. She is resting right now; however, I know she would love to see you. Please come in." Joseph looked back at Ahanu, "Are you coming in?" He explained, "This is my friend I am staying with for a few days. Ahanu, this is Harvey." Ahanu shook Harvey's hand, but Harvey leaned over and hugged him. "I am so happy that you have Joseph staying with you. He is a Godsend."

Joseph and Ahanu entered the house. All the lights were out, so Harvey explained, "Please accept my apologies for the darkness. The doctors want Amitola to rest but without bright lights." Joseph approached Amitola, "Hello Amitola. I just wanted to come by and check on you." Amitola smiled, "Joseph. I have been waiting for you. I have dreamt of you for years." Joseph was a little surprised and asked, "For years?" Amitola replied, "Yes, for about three years. I dream the same dream at least once a month."

Joseph asked, "Can you share the dream?" Amitola smiled, "Of course. My husband and I are driving in a blizzard. I see a bright light and think that it is a car. However, the blizzard lets up. I see you walking towards us. You walk right beside me and extend your hand to me. Suddenly I am standing outside the car, and you take my hand. My husband is now standing next to me. You are still holding my hand and lead us to an area where the grass is green, and flowers are blooming — no more snowstorm. As we walk with you, I see Jesus. He is smiling at us. He says something, but I can't hear him. I wake up before I hear what he says." Joseph asks, "Did you ever hear from God what your dream means?" Amitola replies, "No, but I know you are to show us the way." Harvey softly speaks up, "She had never shared this dream with me until today at the hospital. She said that you were the man she's been dreaming of for years. When Amitola told me about her dream, I knew you were to save her today. If you had not come along,

I am unsure how long she would have laid in the driveway. I don't normally hear neighbors move around until seven."

Joseph asked, "Amitola, do you know why you fell?" Amitola replied, "Please call me Ami. No, I just saw a bright light, and boom. I was on the ground." Joseph commented, "I am surprised that you are home." Amitola laughed, "By the time I arrived at the hospital, I was much better. They ran tests and found nothing, but they dismissed me because I insisted on coming home." Harvey added, "When she makes up her mind, there is no changing it. She had a dream and saw this house, so we moved here just a month ago." Joseph smiled, "Well, we need to be obedient to God. We don't want to overstay our visit today. I know you need to rest."

Ahanu stood up. "Joseph insisted on checking on you. He was quite worried about you." Joseph added, "Not worried. I wanted to make sure you were okay." Amitola replied, "I wanted to make sure I saw you again. That's why I wanted to come home." Harvey smiled, "Oh, that's why! I thought it was because you wanted to be home with me." Amitola smiled at her husband, "You know I love you. Joseph, will you please come back again." Joseph smiled, "I will be happy to come to see you every day I am here, if that's okay." Harvey replied, "You are welcome here anytime." Amitola added, "I feel like I know you." Joseph smiled, "I felt the same way this morning. I will try to come back tomorrow. We have a family reunion, so not sure what time we will return." Amitola asked, "Can you come before you leave?" Joseph replied, "We leave at nine in the morning. I would hate to awaken you." Harvey answered, "We are normally up at four, so anytime is good." Joseph smiled, "Okay, I will come by on my jog." Harvey replied, "Perfect. I will make some coffee." Joseph replied, "Thank you, but I don't drink coffee." Amitola laughed, "I drink cocoa. Do you?" Joseph smiled, "I sure do. I will see you for cocoa in the morning."

Harvey walked the men to the door, "I am so happy you came by. Did you notice how she lit up when you entered the room?" Joseph asked, "Is she okay?" Harvey replied, "Yes, she is. She is just exhausted. It was a busy day of blood draws, tests, and x-rays. Everything checked out perfectly. It was your prayer this morning. Thank you again." Joseph hugged Harvey, "I am glad I was obedient to God prompting me to come in this direction. See you in the morning."

The men drove home in silence; each was processing the visit. Ahanu was the first to speak, "Wow. The Creator is amazing. I have never had anyone tell me they dreamt of me for years." Joseph replied, "I am astonished. Yah, all the honor and glory are Yours. You are the King of kings. The Lord of lords. You are El Elyon, the Most High Elohim. There is no one like You." Joseph parked in front of Ahanu's house, "I can't wait to see what He tells me about Amitola and Harvey. But for now, let's enjoy Sophia and Joey." Ahanu nodded in agreement.

They walked into a full house. Sophia, Joey, and Lucy had arrived. Isabella greeted them, "Where did you guys disappear to? I was getting ready to text you." Joseph smiled, "Sorry, I took a detour home and stopped to see a new friend." Lucy walked up, "That does not surprise me. Joseph and Ahanu, this is my mother, Debbie." The men greeted her, "It is a pleasure to meet you." Debbie responded, "I am sure the pleasure is mine. Thank you both for being so kind to my daughter." Joseph greeted Sophia as she joined the group, "Sophia, this is my good friend and brother Ahanu." Sophia replied, "Thank you for inviting us to your beautiful home. Joey is in the backyard with Meekaila." Ahanu answered, "I am happy that you could join us. I am finding myself being very selfish in wanting to be with Joseph." Sophia laughed, "I am afraid that it seems everyone feels the same way about this young man." Joseph bashfully replied, "It is God who shines through me. I need to see my buddy, Joey. If you will excuse me, I will go find him."

Joseph stepped out into the backyard, and the kids immediately saw him. They came running at him. Meekaila screamed, "Uncle Joey, where have you been?" Joey jumped into Joseph's arms, "I missed you, best friend!" Joseph laughed, "I missed you both! Have you been having fun?" Joey replied, "Yes, we have. I am glad you invited us to come to Meekaila's house. She is my new best friend." Joseph added, "I knew you would become best friends."

The rest of the adults joined them outside. Ahanu headed to the grill, "The burgers and dogs will be ready soon. Who's hungry?" Meekaila and Joey yelled in unison, "I am!" Sophia walked up to Joseph, "I don't know how you did it, but Joey has come out of his shell." Joseph smiled, "I didn't do anything. God is working on him." Sophia replied, "He suddenly has so much confidence. He is full of life again. Thank you." Joseph smiled, "I am happy to help in any way I can. I meant it. God is working every day. We just have to be obedient." Sophia suddenly hugged Joseph and whispered, "Thank you, Joseph. Finally, I have my little boy back. I didn't know how to get him back." Joseph whispered back, "He is an awesome little boy. I thank God for his friendship."

As the adults gathered around the picnic table, the kids played on the swings. Isabella, Lucy, and Sophia placed all the food on the table. Suddenly Ahanu hollered, "Ready or not, burgers and dogs are ready." Meekaila and Joey ran to the table. The kids hurried to Joseph and sat next to him. They grabbed plates and served themselves, so Joseph grabbed a hotdog and reached for the Mac and Cheese. "I heard this is world-class famous, so I need to make sure Joey doesn't eat it all before I get some." Joey laughed, "I love Mac and Cheese." Meekaila chimed in, "I do too. It is my favorite!" Isabella laughed, "Should we say grace before we eat?" Joseph laughed with a mouth full, "I guess I was hungrier than I thought." Joey had a mouth full of Mac and Cheese, "Me too!" Ahanu shook his head, "I see why you are both named Joey. I will say grace. Thank you, Jesus, for this time together. Bless all my new family. Amen." Meekaila giggled, "Jesus come to eat with us. Amen."

Joseph and Joey were laughing. They were having a contest to see who would finish their hotdog first. Meekaila said, "Daddy, both Joey's are racing. Can I join them?" Isabella laughed, "I am surprised you haven't beaten them." Ahanu smiled at Meekaila, "Go ahead, honey. Beat the boys." Meekaila giggled and began to gobble up her hotdog. The race was a tight one, but Joseph would not allow two little kids to win. Joseph took the last bite, chewed fiercely, then swallowed and shouted, "I win!" Everyone exploded in laughter.

Joseph noticed that Debbie was not talking much, so he sat beside her. He asked, "Debbie may I pray for you?" Debbie looked at him quite surprised, "Why would you?" Joseph smiled, "I hear the Lord saying that you need some peace." Debbie replied, "Sure. I guess I shouldn't ever refuse prayer." Joseph smiled, "Heavenly Father, thank you for bringing Debbie to join us today in celebrating and glorifying You. Thank you for bringing peace to her. Open her eyes to see the beauty that you see." Joseph squeezed Debbie's hand, "I release peace in Jesus' Name." Debbie felt a sense of peace come over her that she had never felt before. Debbie looked at Joseph with tears, "Thank you, Joseph. I see why my daughter is so enamored with you. You do carry an anointing that I have not experienced before. Thank you for being obedient."

Sophia had been watching and listening to Debbie and Joseph. She asked, "Joseph, can you pray for me too." Joseph smiled, "I would be honored to." When Joey noticed that his mommy was asking for prayer, he went and stood next to her. Joseph sat beside her and softly spoke to her, "I hear the Lord saying, 'My beautiful daughter, your womb is blessed; your son is my servant. Things are going to change for you. I am sending an abundance of blessings your way. Receive My peace. I am releasing an abundance of wealth to you. Receive it. I am sending a messenger to guide you. I am also bringing someone into your life that will be a daddy to your son. Joey knows what he looks like and who he is. Trust Me. Doubt is not from Me. Rebuke it when it comes around, and it must flee. Have faith; I have been watching over you and Joey all your lives." Sophia softly replied, "I receive it." Joseph continued, "Abba Father, thank you. Sophia, I impart to you a new level of love. I also activate your seeing gift in Jesus' name." Joseph was looking at Sophia, "Sophia, open your eyes." Sophia opened her eyes, and tears began to flow. She said, "I had never seen such beauty. I can see the guardian angels for everyone. Also, all the colors are more vibrant." Joey smiled, "Yes, mommy. Isn't it beautiful?" Joey threw his arms around her and laughed. Sophia cried, "Thank you for being so kind and obedient." Joseph replied, "The Kingdom of Heaven is at hand."

The afternoon flew by, full of laughter and great conversations. Joey and Sophia found an extended family. Debbie learned that she was no better or different from those not the same as her. The peace Debbie felt she would work to keep forever. She had a fantastic time and blended in without a problem. Lucy knew she was home with her new family. Just like that, it was dinnertime.

Meekaila and Joey were the first to notice that it was dinnertime. They came and asked, "Can we have more hotdogs?" Ahanu glanced at his watch, "Oh gosh. Time to eat again. Shall we make more dogs and burgers, or should I bring some steaks?" The kids yelled, "Hotdogs, hotdogs, please!" Isabella laughed, "The kids can have hot dogs, but I think we should have steaks." So, Ahanu and Isabella went into the house for steaks. They exited the house with a tray of steaks and veggies. Joseph jumped up, "Can I help?" Isabella replied, "Yes, please." She handed him her tray. Joseph followed Ahanu to the grill.

Joseph and Ahanu began to grill dinner. They enjoyed their time together, teasing one another. Ahanu whispered, "I think you and Lucy would be great together." Joseph teased back, "Well, I think Isabella is ready for another baby." Ahanu laughed, "Well, that would be up to her. I have wanted another, but she still struggles. Well, you know." Joseph was now serious, "I know. I hear the Lord saying it is time. I can hear laughter. No, it is giggling. Ahanu, you will have a boy."

Isabella had snuck up behind the men, "What are you guys whispering?" Joseph turned and smiled. "May I pray for you?" Isabella replied, "Of course, you can." Joseph placed one hand on her shoulder and asked her to put her hand on her womb. He then placed his hand over hers. Tears immediately started to flow down her cheeks.

Joseph began, "Creator, You are the King of kings. The beginning and the end. The Aleph and the Tav. You knew us before we came to earth. We swam in Your River of Life before you sent us to earth. Thank you for my sister, Isabella. Creator says the time has come. No more mourning. It is a time for healing. Your precious son is a blessing in heaven. He loves to sing, and I will bless you with another son. He too will love to sing." Isabella was now crying aloud. Joseph continued, "I speak healing to your heart and your womb in Jesus' name. Be healed and made whole." Ahanu embraced his wife, and they cried. Joseph placed his hand on Ahanu, too, "This bond that Creator knit together will not be broken. Healing for you as individuals but, more importantly, as a couple. A covenant partnership. A covenant with God. The blood of Yeshua covers you and your entire family. Thank you, Yah!"

Joseph turned to watch the steaks. He had tears streaming down his cheeks. Suddenly, he felt both the kids hugging him. He looked down at them, and they were crying. He knelt and hugged them. "Are you okay?" he asked. The kids smiled and nodded their heads. In unison, they said, "We love Uncle Joey." Joseph replied, "I love you too." Joseph stood up, "How about you help me get plates on the table. I will put the steaks and veggies on the table." Meekaila and Joey ran to get more paper plates."

As they sat for dinner, Meekaila and Joey asked to say grace. Meekaila started, "Thank you, Jesus, for our new bigger family." Joey added, "Thank you, Jesus, for all this delicious food." Then, in unison, everyone said, "Amen."

Chapter 21 Cinnamon Rolls and Cocoa

Joseph awoke early. Before getting out of bed, he said his prayer, "Yah, thank you for another day to honor and glorify You. Thank You for the wonderful family that You have blessed and given me. I ask for and receive an abundance of grace today. All I need in my life is You. You have blessed me beyond measure. Yah let's have some more fun today. No limits, Yah!" Joseph heard the Lord chuckle. 'No limits, son.'

It was the family reunion day and his cocoa date with Harvey and Amitola. Joseph dressed in his running clothes, and out the door he headed. Joseph took a deep breath as he arrived at Harvey and Amitola's; the aroma of cocoa was overpowering. He rang the doorbell and waited. Harvey came to the door, "Good morning, Joseph. Come on in." Joseph replied, "Good morning. How's Ami?" Harvey answered, "Why don't you tell me?" Amitola stood up, "Joseph! I am so glad you made it. I made you some cinnamon rolls this morning." Joseph replied, "Oh my! You must have gotten up early today." Harvey replied first, "She couldn't sleep, so she baked for you." Amitola laughed, "Yes, that's true, but I had some help." Harvey laughed, "We both are thrilled to have you here."

Joseph teased, "If I had known that cinnamon rolls were waiting for me, I would have come earlier." Amitola laughed, "I could have had you help me make them and let Harvey rest." Harvey jumped in, "Hold on now. Making cinnamon rolls has always been our fun time together." Joseph replied, "How long have you made cinnamon rolls together?" Harvey smiled at his wife, "Twenty years ago, we made our first rolls." Amitola laughed, "Actually, it was twenty-one years ago. We made some together before we got married. Remember? I was getting ready to meet your parents, and I wanted to bring something along." Harvey smiled, "Oh yeah. How could I have forgotten that disaster?"

Joseph asked, "Disaster? Tell me about it." Amitola laughed, "It wasn't a true disaster; the rolls came out wonderful. The rolls were huge and delicious. We got into a little accident on our way to his parents, and the rolls did not survive. I ended up meeting his parents at the hospital." Joseph asked, "Clearly, you were okay, but how bad was the accident?" Harvey answered, "Someone ran a red light and hit us on the passenger side. It was clear that an angel protected Ami. According to the police reports and doctors, Ami should not have survived." Amitola continued the story, "I only had a few cuts and bruises. Harvey decided that if I could survive that accident, I could survive anything. He proposed to me that day." Harvey laughed, "Well, I was pretty high on drugs that day. I suffered more injuries than Ami. My story is that I did not know what I was doing due to the drugs. Miss Ami would not let me out of the agreement." Joseph chuckled. "I can tell that you have a fantastic marriage. Do you have children?" Amitola smiled, "We do have two sons. Benjamin is at Pepperdine. And our younger son Eli is at the University of Pennsylvania. Both interested in medicine." Joseph replied, "Wow. You must be very proud of them." Harvey answered, "We are very proud. They are both awesome sons. We see them often." Amitola laughed, "We live smack in the middle, so we can hop on a plane to visit anytime I get too lonely."

Amitola said, "Enough about us; tell us about yourself. I want to know why I dream of you so often." Joseph began, "I will give you the short version; a loving mom adopted me. She went home to heaven when I was seven, and occasionally I can still smell her fragrance. When I was a freshman in high school, my dad died. I moved in with my uncle. He was nice enough, but I never felt like I was home. My track coach was my father figure through high school. He took me under his wing. I went off to college and didn't return very often. I worked through college, and when I graduated, I was fortunate enough to join a consulting company. I am still with the same company. I was recently made a partner, so I am doing well for myself." Amitola responded,

"You tell your story as if every graduate gets offered a great job." Joseph replied, "I don't believe that was all me. I understand and have seen the favor throughout my life. I didn't notice it until recently."

Harvey asked, "Joseph, you must have had a complicated life. How are you?" Joseph chuckled, "I am so much better than most people. My family continues to grow almost daily." Amitola responded, "I see why. You are a special young man. I see it all over you." Joseph asked, "Are you believers in YAHUAH?" Harvey replied, "Yes. We have been living a Godly life since we got married." Joseph replied, "That is so good to hear. Ami, can we talk about your dream?" Amitola answered, "Yes. I want to know why I dream about you." Joseph asked, "Have you gotten any clarity?"

Amitola glanced at Harvey, "Before my youngest son went away to college, I began to dream about you almost every day. I asked God what the dream meant, but I never really felt I got clarity." Joseph replied, "I was expecting to get some clarity too, but I didn't hear anything. Can we pray together and see if Yah gives us anything?" Harvey replied, "Yes, let's pray." Amitola asked, "Joseph would you mind leading the prayer?" Joseph replied, "Absolutely. It would be my pleasure and honor." Joseph reached over and held Amitola and Harvey's hands.

Joseph felt electricity run through his hands into theirs. He felt Amitola jerk. She opened her eyes and asked, "What was that?" Joseph reassured her, "That is the Holy Spirit. He is doing something in us all."

Harvey still had his eyes closed. "I see the most beautiful rainbow. I can honestly say that I have never seen colors so bright. The colors appear to be singing." Joseph smiled, "That's great! We have not even started praying. See how God works." Amitola squeezed Joseph's hand and closed her eyes.

Joseph began to pray, "Abba, Father, El Elyon, You are the beginning and the End. You are worthy of all praise. You are the only true living God. You are the Creator of all things. You created the heavens, the earth, the stars, and galaxies. You breathed life into Adam. You are Omnipotent. You are the God of Abraham, Isaac, and Jacob, our forefathers. I thank You, Yah, for putting Ami and Harvey in my life. Your Word says that You are here among us where two or more gather in Your Name. Thank You for Your presence. Holy Spirit, we invite you to minister to us. Heavenly Host, fight any battles that may be raging around us. Papa, we seek You and ask that You show us clarity to this dream that Your precious daughter Ami has been having. Not our will but Your Will, Lord. Thank you, Papa, for Your Son, Yahushuah HaMashiach. Thank You, Jesus, for your love for us." Joseph continued to pray silently in his spiritual language.

Amitola began to cry. Joseph watched her closely. Harvey opened his eyes, "Are you okay, honey?" Amitola opened her eyes and looked at her husband, "Yes, I am just fine." She looked at Joseph as she softly spoke, "The Lord showed me a vision of all that you have suffered. I saw your mother's death and the pain you endured for many years in the vision. He also showed me the day that He came to you again. His message to you is, My son, all will be revealed to you soon." Joseph smiled, "Yes, that is a confirmation. I receive that Word."

Harvey was next to speak, "I hear the Lord say, there are promises for you that He will reveal to you soon. My plans are not man's plans. You are My multifaceted diamond. I will open many doors for you that no man or demon can close. What I open, no one closes. Attah, yachiyd Yoceph." Harvey looked at Joseph, a little puzzled. Harvey said, "I have no idea how I said those words. I do not speak any other languages." Joseph laughed, "Well, those are prophetic words God put in you to speak. The last words you spoke are Hebrew. They mean, 'Thou art my beloved son Joseph.' I have heard them before." Harvey replied, "I have never given a prophetic word before. That is awesome. Will I continue to do this?" Joseph replied, "As long as you are obedient to God's voice. When He prompts you, then step out in faith."

Joseph looked at Amitola, "Are you okay?" Amitola nodded yes. Joseph continued, "God works in mysterious ways. We were seeking Him for the dream, and He has you both prophesy to me." Amitola smiled, "Have you had others prophesy to you?" Joseph thought, "No,

I can't say that I have. I usually pray for people and teach them what Ruach Haqodesh, the Holy Spirit, has taught me." Amitola replied, "For today, I believe this is what God wanted. Maybe the next time we meet, He will reveal more about the dream." Joseph agreed, "I think you may be correct. All I see and know is that we will continue to be connected. I see Harvey's faith growing, and Ami, I still can't shake the feeling of knowing you." Amitola smiled, "Me neither. I know there is more, but I don't have clarity. I have also dreamt of you for three years, so you are familiar to me."

Harvey added, "Not to change the conversation, but what are your plans for today and the next few days?" Joseph replied, "I am going to Ahanu's family reunion. I hope to see my natural mother there." Amitola asked, "Why do you believe you will see her?" Joseph answered, "I don't know for sure, but Ahanu and I look so much alike that we believe my mother must be related to him."

Amitola sighed, "How will you feel if she doesn't want to acknowledge you as her child?" Joseph replied, "I would walk away from her. She wouldn't be worthy of having me as her son. It would end my desire to be in her life. However, I would still have Ahanu as my brother and friend. I would also have an extended family that truly loves me. So, you see, I win either way." Both Harvey and Amitola were smiling at Joseph. Amitola smiled, "Joseph, you are a special young man. If your mother refuses to be in your life, she is a foolish woman."

Joseph glanced at his watch, "I am so sorry to leave in a rush, but I need to get back. We leave for the reunion in an hour." Harvey asked, "Can I give you a ride?" Joseph smiled, "Thank you. I can make the run back. It's only a few blocks away." Amitola asked, "Will you come back tomorrow and tell us all about the reunion?" Joseph smiled, "Yes. I would love that."

Amitola and Harvey walked Joseph to the door. As Joseph jogged back, he thought about the prophetic words that he had received. He asked, 'Papa, why am I in Ami's life?' Joseph heard Papa audibly say, 'Wait and see, My son.'

Zephaniah 3:16-17

In that day it will be said to Jerusalem:
"Do not be afraid, O Zion;
Do not let your hands fall limp.
¹⁷

"The LORD your God is in your midst,
A Warrior who saves.
He will rejoice over you with joy;
He will be quiet in His love [making no mention of your past
sins],
He will rejoice over you with shouts of joy.

Chapter 22 The Reunion

As they arrived at the reunion, Joseph was very excited and expecting big things. He met many people that did look a little like him. He met lawyers, doctors, educators, grandparents, fathers and mothers, college students, and many little ones. All were very welcoming and gracious. He searched the crowd for the face he remembered seeing. As people greeted him, he searched their faces for any resemblance.

As they prepared to sit down to eat, he noticed a child sitting alone. He approached him, "Hello, may I sit with you?" The little boy smiled, "Hi. My name is Wamblee." Joseph smiled at him, "It is great to meet you, Wamblee. I love your name!" Wamblee explained, "My nickname is Little Eagle." Joseph responded, "Oh, I see. I like both of your names. I am Joseph." Wamblee asked, "What is your real name?" Joseph replied, "That is my real name. I don't have another." Wamblee smiled, "I will give you a name." Joseph replied, "Okay. What do you think my name should be?"

Wamblee thought, then announced, "You are Wamblee Taaraka." Joseph asked, "I like it. What does it mean?" Wamblee responded, "Wamblee means eagle. Taaraka means three things; star, eye, and Savior." Joseph asked, "Which one do you believe is the meaning?" Wamblee looked at Joseph and stared at him. Wamblee spoke very deliberately, "I see a star over your head. When I saw you the first time, I saw an eye. I believe that your name will take many meanings. To some, you will be Eagle Eye. To others, you will be a savior. Creator sees you as His bright and shining star." Joseph asked, "How do you see me?" Wamblee smiled, "I see you like an eagle flying high, and you have your eye on the people that Creator shows you." Joseph watched Wamblee, "Little Eagle, you are wise beyond your years." Wamblee replied, "I hear Creator, which makes many people afraid of me. You walked right up to me without fear."

Joseph replied, "I am not afraid of you. I hear Creator too, and He highlighted you sitting alone. Creator told me that most people misunderstand you. He said you needed a friend. May I be your friend?" Wamblee smiled, "Yes. I knew that you were going to be my friend. I had a dream about you last night." Joseph asked, "Really? What was the dream about?" Wamblee shared, "I saw you like an eagle flying high almost to heaven. You told me you would show me how to know when Creator spoke to me. You said that sometimes I hear the darkness. I then saw a big raven, and you killed it." Joseph smiled, "I see how Creator shows you things. If you are not fearful, you too can kill the ravens." Wamblee replied, "Sometimes I have bad dreams. What should I do?"

Joseph felt sympathy for Wamblee. Joseph said, "I am sorry you have bad dreams. When you fall asleep and awaken, ask Creator to protect you. Then, you can say, the blood of the Son of the Creator, Yahushuah HaMashiach covers me." Wamblee laughed, "I know Him. He sometimes comes into my dreams and talks to me. He is my friend. I hear angels call Him, the Word." Joseph smiled, "Yes. That is His name. People call him by many names. Some call Him Yeshua. Some Yahusha. Some Yahushuah. Some Jesus. In every language, they interpret His name differently. It doesn't matter what people call Him. You must call Him by the name He asks you to use." Wamblee smiled, "Wamblee Taaraka, you are very wise. Thank you for being my friend." Joseph put his hand on Wamblee's head, "I am honored to have such a wise young friend."

Meekaila walked up to Joseph, "Uncle Joey, I see you met my cousin Wamblee. Hello Wamblee." Wamblee smiled, "Hello, Meekaila. Wamblee Taaraka is my new friend." Meekaila laughed, "Uncle Joey, you have a new name. Wamblee Taaraka. I love it!" Joseph replied, "I am so glad you do. Wamblee gave it to me." Meekaila responded, "Wamblee, you gave him a perfect name."

Joseph asked, "Meekaila, will you be sitting with us?" Meekaila smiled, "Of course. I have to sit with you, Uncle Joey." Wamblee laughed, "I am happy you are sitting with us, Meekaila. Is your mom bringing you food?" Meekaila replied, "No, she is not; I can get my food. I was waiting for Uncle Joey." Suddenly Wamblee behaved like a small child, "Come on guys, let's go get some food." So, they headed to the buffet line.

Joseph was still looking at everyone's faces. Wamblee pulled at his arm, "She is not here. Stop looking." Joseph looked down at Wamblee, "What? How do you know?" Wamblee replied, "Creator said she could not come. She was not feeling well." Joseph looked down, almost feeling discouraged. Meekaila said, "Uncle Joey? Don't feel sad." Joseph smiled at her, "I am not sad. I am here with you and Wamblee. I am most definitely happy."

Joseph helped the two young ones serve their plates. He loaded his plate with lots of veggies. The kids made faces when he offered them veggies. Finally, Meekaila said, "We don't have to eat veggies today. We are on vacation." Joseph laughed, "I'm sorry. I didn't realize you could take a vacation from veggies." Wamblee laughed, "Me too. I am on vacation."

Joseph asked Wamblee as they sat down, "Wamblee, where are your parents?" Wamblee looked around, then pointed them out, "Do you see the man wearing the white clothes?" Joseph answered, "Yes." Wamblee replied, "That's my daddy. Look over there. See the lady with a headdress on her head?" Joseph looked in the direction that Wamblee pointed, "Yes. Is that your mom?" Wamblee answered, "Yes, she is. Mommy is so pretty." Joseph responded, "Yes, she is." Wamblee added, "My daddy is Gabby, a hero of God. My mommy is Tabassum; she is Smiling Flower." Joseph smiled, "I see that their names are quite fitting. I can see your daddy has much authority. Your mommy is beautiful and has a beautiful smile too."

Meekaila asked, "Uncle Joey, what do you see for Wamblee?" Joseph glanced at Meekaila, then back at Wamblee, "I see a brave young man. He sees as well as an eagle. His hearing is very sharp. He is wise beyond his years." Meekaila asked, "What do you see about me?"

Joseph turned to look at Meekaila, "I see a messenger of joy and laughter. I see you as a vessel that pours out joy." Meekaila asked, "What is a vessel?" Joseph laughed, "Sorry, Meekaila, it is like a pitcher. I see you pouring joy upon everyone. I see joy and wisdom." The two kids smiled at each other. Wamblee said, "I have never had anyone say that to me." Meekaila chimed in, "Me either!"

Gabby and Tabassum walked up as the two kids laughed. "What's so funny?" They asked. Wamblee replied, "Mommy, Joseph told Meekaila that she is a pitcher pouring out joy." Tabassum smiled, "I can see that." Meekaila added, "Wamblee is old." Joseph laughed, "I did not say old. I said Wamblee is wise beyond his years." Gabby chuckled, "Yes, he is. I am always astonished at the things he says."

Joseph stood up, "I am Joseph. How are you doing?" Gabby replied, "Nice to meet you, Joseph. We have heard many wonderful things about you." Tabassum added, "I hope you are feeling welcomed." Joseph replied, "I sure am. Will you be joining us?" He encouraged the kids to make room. "Let's squeeze together so others can sit here." The kids were giggling.

Gabby sat down, "You look so much like Ahanu. He tells us you're adopted. Do you know anything about your birth parents?" Joseph replied, "Not really; I only know what Creator has shown me." Tabassum asked, "What is that?" Joseph glanced at the kids, "I just know my mom was very young, scared, and alone." Gabby and Tabassum understood what he meant. Tabassum cautiously replied, "I see. She must have been terrified. I hope you find her." Gabby asked, "How long have you looked for her? Have you looked for your dad?" Joseph replied, "No, I have not looked for him. I just started looking for my mom. I don't know names or locations. All I know is that I was born in the Midwest. I have never seen my birth certificate." Wamblee reminded Joseph, "Remember, I told you she is not here. She was not feeling well." Joseph smiled at Wamblee, "Yes, I remember. I did stop looking when you told me."

Gabby asked, "What exactly are you looking for?" Joseph replied, "I was looking for others that look like Ahanu and myself." Gabby laughed, "Well, I think most of us look alike." Joseph responded, "Yes but not exactly alike. Ahanu and I look like twins but twenty years difference." Gabby chuckled, "Yes, I did notice that." Tabassum asked, "Joseph, do you have anything else to go by?" Joseph responded, "I know when I see her, I will know it is her." Tabassum asked, "How can you be so sure?" Joseph replied, "I don't know how to explain it other than the Ruach Haqodesh, the Holy Spirit, or Great Spirit gives me an understanding or knowing about things."

Wamblee interjected, "Mommy, he hears and sees Creator as I do. He has also seen the Word." Tabassum smiled at her son, "Oh, I see. He too, is like you?" Tabassum looked at Joseph, "When Wamblee first started speaking of Creator and the Word we were concerned. We went to many medicine men seeking answers. Finally, Wamblee told us that they did not understand because they had never really seen the True Creator and the Truth, the Word." Joseph replied, "Wow! Truly wise beyond your years. It reminds me of the scripture where Yahushuah HaMashiach asks Peter who he believed He was. And Peter says the Son of God, The Messiah. Yahushuah said that it was the Ruach or Spirit of God that gave him that revelation."

Tabassum continued, "We thought he must be going crazy or attacked by some demon. The medicine men refused to give us a remedy to fix him. They just said they could do nothing. They couldn't even look at our son." Joseph again replied, "Wow." Tabassum continued, "You can see our concern for our child. He was not like the other children. He could tell us things that no one else could explain. Finally, one day we ran into a man on the street that spoke these words. Stop seeking man and start asking God for answers. He then walked away and disappeared. We looked down at our child and then back to him when he walked away, but he had disappeared." Joseph softly said, "Yah sent a messenger to you." Tabassum agreed, "Yes, I agree. From that day forward, we started to pray like never before. We were not praying people before that experience. After that, we have had many supernatural encounters." Joseph was smiling, "That's awesome."

Gabby replied, "As an elder, it was hard to understand or put my mind around everything happening to us. However, we, too, had an understanding and knowledge of what the truth was. We have a son that sees the Creator; not all children do, or even adults. We need to be obedient to what we hear Creator tell us. We have one of His gifts that we must care for and cherish. We do not take that lightly." Joseph smiled, "I understand. From this day forward, you will see growth in your son. Everyone he meets will like him. I see him having many very good friends. He will be popular and a blessing to others. Yes, I hear a blessing to others is emphasized."

Gabby had tears running down his face. He responded, "I receive those words for my son." Joseph placed his hand on Wamblee's head, "Papa, bless this child and his parents. May they experience even more of Your supernatural life. I hear Creator saying, Wamblee walk with Me. I will continue to lead you. Come with me to higher places that not many have experienced." Joseph looked at Gabby and Tabassum and lightly touched their shoulders, "Have faith. Be made whole in the name of Yahushuah HaMashiach." They fell under the Spirit and Power of Yah. They began to speak in unknown tongues. Wamblee whispered to Joseph, "Now, they will have even more understanding." Joseph nodded his head in agreement and whispered, "Yep, I agree."

Ahanu had made his way to the group just as Gabby and Tabassum began to speak in unknown tongues. He felt the Ruach Haqodesh come upon him and began interpreting the languages. "It is time for my people to arise. It is time for them to hear MY Words. I AM the GREAT I AM. I AM THE CREATOR! THE CREATOR OF ALL THINGS. I AM THE SAME YESTERDAY, TODAY AND FOREVER! I have chosen you from the beginning of time. I chose you for such a time as this. ARISE, MIGHTY WARRIORS! ARISE, MIGHTY WARRIORS! Do not step to the left or the right without my prompting. DO YOU HEAR ME? ARISE, MIGHTY WARRIORS! ARISE, MIGHTY WARRIORS! I am calling you forth. ARISE DRY BONES!"

Suddenly Joseph felt the entire place get hot. He saw fire come down. He quickly asked, 'Papa is this you?' The reply was swift, 'Yes, son.' Meekaila and Wamblee were giggling. Joseph looked around the room, and people were falling on the floor. He could tell that they were under the Spirit of the Lord and the Fire of the Holy Spirit. Laughter broke out. Suddenly Wamblee pulled at Joseph's hand. Wamblee whispered, "She is coming." Joseph asked, "Who?" Wamblee whispered, "Your mommy." Joseph asked, "When?" Meekaila giggled, "She is walking to her car. I see her. She is wearing a purple dress." Wamblee agreed, "Yes, it is a purple dress. It has little tiny white flowers. She is beautiful. She looks like you." Joseph smiled, "Thank you, Yah!"

Joseph, Meekaila, and Wamblee began to sing a song prophetically inspired by the Holy Spirit. "Oh, how He loves me. My Savior came and gave His life for me. Oh, how He loves me. Oh, how He loves me. He is the King of kings. He is the Lord of lords. Oh, how He loves me. Oh, how He loves me. He is the One and Only True Living God. He is the One and Only, True and Living Yah. Oh, how He loves me. Oh, how He loves me. He chose me; He chose me. Oh, how He loves me. Oh, how He loves me. Oh, how He loves me. He is the GREAT I AM. He is the GREAT I AM. Oh, how He loves me. Oh, how He loves me. Oh, how He loves me. Oh, how He loves me. He truly loves me."

Joseph looked around, and all the people were worshipping the King. He laughed as he noticed some people would begin to sit up and fall over again — the children were all laughing with heavenly joy. The joy of the Lord continued for quite some time. Joseph continued to sing praises and worship the King. He sang, "For you are worthy of being praised. You are my Lord and Yah! You are worthy to receive all the glory! You are worthy to receive all the honor and power. You created all things because of Your will; they exist. Because of Your will, they were created and brought into being. You are the GREAT I AM. The Sovereign King."

Suddenly, Joseph could hear the heavenly hosts singing, "HOLY, HOLY, HOLY is the LORD GOD, THE ALMIGHTY, the Omnipotent, the Ruler of all, WHO WAS AND WHO IS AND WHO IS TO COME, the unchanging, eternal God." Then he began to hear in Hebrew, "KADOSH, KADOSH, KADOSH, ADONAI EL ELYON, KADOSH, KADOSH, KADOSH, ADONAI ELOHIM TZ'VA'OT, ADONAI ELOHIM TZ'VA'OT, 'ERETS MELO KABOWD,

KADOSH, KADOSH, KADOSH, KADOSH, KADOSH, KADOSH, HAYAH
HAYAH, HAYAH HAYAH, KADOSH, KADOSH, KADOSH, EL SHADDAI,
KADOSH, KADOSH, KADOSH." Which Joseph understood to mean,
"Holy, Holy, Holy, the Most High Elohim, Holy, Holy, Holy, Yahuah
Elohim of hosts, the whole earth is full of glory. Holy, Holy, Holy, Holy,
Holy, Holy, Yahuah, Yahuah (I AM THAT I AM), Holy, Holy, Holy, God
Almighty, Holy, Holy, Holy."

Wamblee came and stood next to Joseph. Joseph asked, "Do you hear
them?" Wamblee replied, "Yes. They are beautiful." Meekaila had
joined them, "Yes, they are." Joseph smiled at the kids. They stood in
silence as they listened. It went on for quite some time. People were
standing and worshipping, some in various unknown tongues, some in
their Native language, some in English, and some in Spanish. The
sound was beautifully blended. When it seemed that it would end,
someone would startup in a solo; then others joined in.

Joseph closed his eyes to enjoy the singing. He felt he was lifted into
the heavens. Joseph had no idea that he was above the floor. He
continued to enjoy the sound and joined in the worship. Meekaila
started to giggle. Wamblee saw Joseph lifted. Wamblee asked, "Can I
do that too?" Joseph didn't open his eyes but reached for Wamblee,
but when he didn't feel him, he opened his eyes and searched for
Wamblee. Joseph noticed that Wamblee and Meekaila were about
two feet below him. He was surprised but not shocked. He began to
laugh. He slowly lowered to the floor. Wamblee asked again, "Can I
do that?" Joseph replied, "I am sure you can. I don't know how it
happened." Meekaila laughed, "I saw an angel hold you by the
shoulders." Joseph responded, "I did feel something on my shoulders
but thought it was the presence of Yah." Joseph added, "I didn't see
the angels. I only heard them." Wamblee replied, "I saw them and
heard them. I also saw the Word." Joseph replied, "That is awesome.
Meekaila, did you see something?" Meekaila asked, "Besides the angel
that was holding your shoulders?" Joseph smiled, "Yes. Besides that."
Meekaila continued, "I also saw Jesus and the angels. When Jesus
entered the room, they all fell on their faces and worshipped Him."

Ahanu was listening, "I saw nothing but heard everything." Others started to share their experiences. One lady saw the throne and God. She could not make out His face but saw a brilliant light shining from the throne." Another lady described the flowers that she saw. "The flowers were alive and singing and worshipping the Lord." Meekaila's Uncle Pete explained, "I have never experienced anything like this. How do I continue to experience this peace that I feel?" Joseph replied, "Walk with God! Believe that Jesus is King. Believe that the Son of God is Yahushua HaMashiach. He is Yeshua the only Messiah. Follow Him. Your faith will grow, and you will see many things. You will have supernatural experiences. Worship only God the Father, Yahushua HaMashiach the Son, and Ruach Haqodesh the Holy Spirit. Confess your sins, be baptized by full water immersion to show that you are willing to kill the flesh and be resurrected in Christ. Be willing to receive all that God's Spirit, Ruach Haqodesh, has for you. Read His Word and follow his commands. Be transformed in Christ Jesus the Messiah."

Wamblee pulled at Joseph's hand, "Joseph, she is here." Joseph looked at Wamblee and asked, "Who?" Wamblee smiled, "Your mother." Joseph looked around the room but didn't see anyone new.

The doors opened, and a woman walked in. She had on a long white cardigan. He could not make out her face from across the room. She walked straight to the group, and Ahanu was the first to recognize her. He greeted her, "Hello Amitola. I didn't realize you belonged in the family." She had her eyes fixed on Joseph, "I didn't either until I heard the Lord say, 'Get up and go to the family reunion.' Here I am." Joseph was at a loss for words, "I, I don't understand." Amitola laughed, "You are my baby boy. I had a knowing from the moment I saw you. I needed God to confirm it." Joseph had tears streaming down his face, "I don't understand. You do not look at all like the face I saw in my vision." Amitola laughed, "You look exactly like me, Joseph." Suddenly Ahanu's eyes were opened, "Oh my God. I had not even noticed the resemblance." Joseph was still confused, "I am sorry, but I don't see it." Amitola prayed, "Father, allow him to see. I am asking this in Your Mighty Son's Name, Christ Jesus the Messiah."

Joseph blinked, and he saw Amitola for the first time. "Mom?" Amitola laughed, "Yes, son." Harvey had finally entered the room and made his way to the group. "I am so sorry I missed the initial meeting. I was parking the car. Amitola jumped out and ran inside." Joseph embraced Amitola, "I have missed you so much." Amitola cried, "I have thought about you every day of my life. I was so sorry to have to give you up. I was so afraid and ashamed." Harvey hugged Amitola and Joseph, "I am so happy to meet my son and see my wife with her firstborn." Wamblee interrupted the group hug, "I have to see her dress."

Joseph laughed, "Ami, can you open your cardigan?" Wamblee began to laugh, "She is wearing a purple dress with tiny flowers." Meekaila giggled, "Sorry, Auntie. We both saw your purple dress and had to prove it was you." Amitola laughed, "I see. I am real. I am Joseph's mother."

Joseph grabbed Amitola and led her to a table. "You have to tell me everything." Amitola replied, "You do too." Harvey laughed, "May I start with my part in this. Then maybe we can work backward. How does that sound?" Amitola and Joseph nodded yes in agreement.

Harvey began, "Joseph, on the first day that we met, I saw the resemblance. However, Ami had just fallen, and I was concerned with her health when she told me at the hospital that she had dreamt of you for years. I was shocked because I hadn't heard anything about it. I wondered why. Ami and I have not had any secrets between us. I knew she had had a baby at the age of fifteen. I knew all about the attack. I also saw that she didn't see the resemblance. She thought it was just the dream she had been dreaming. I wanted to say something, but I could tell that you could not see the resemblance, either. Ahanu did not see the resemblance. When I saw the rainbow, I had an understanding that God was answering my prayer for her."

Joseph interrupted, "Yes, the rainbow is the sign of the unbreakable covenant, His promise. That adds such clarity now." Harvey agreed, "That's right. It is God's promise on many levels." He paused a moment, then continued, "In our quiet time together, she always talked about her baby boy. She wondered where you were — wondered if you were safe and healthy. She wondered what you looked like, and now she knows. She had a memory of you but as a baby—a newborn infant. The Lord allowed her always to remember your face. She even took some art classes and had paintings and sketches of you. Which, of course, we didn't show you. Our boys always asked who the baby was, but we kept quiet until three years ago. When we told them about you, they wanted to find you. We attempted to locate you but couldn't find any records of you. It was as if you had just disappeared from the face of the earth. I am ecstatic you found us."

Joseph had tears running down his face. "Yah brought me here. He orchestrated it all. Ahanu also had a lot to do with it. He was obedient to Creator." Joseph asked Amitola, "May I go next?" Amitola nodded yes as tears streamed down her face. She held on tight to Joseph's hand.

Joseph softly began to speak, choking back tears. "I told you that my mom died when I was seven and dad when I was a freshman in high school. Life was hard after mom went home to heaven. Papa came to me and gave me peace for a while. I drifted away from Him due to my circumstances. I missed her hugs and love. As I grew up, my track coach took me under his wing and became the surrogate father I needed. College was a breeze. I worked all four years of college. Initially, I thought the favor I received was all me, but I know better now."

Ami squeezed her son's hand. Joseph smiled at her and continued, "Papa came to me again and told me that he would radically change my life if I followed Him. I didn't have anything to lose. I also knew that my mom loved Papa. Then I started to experience a lot of supernatural things. From people dreaming about me to me dreaming about people I was to meet. I saw many people healed and their lives transformed. Today I experienced being elevated off the floor. Not long ago, I had a vision of you. You were about fourteen or fifteen; I saw what happened to you, not in detail, though. I experienced my conception. I knew that my guardian angel had spoken to you about my safety. I heard Papa's voice at my conception. Hearing His voice is an experience I will never forget. I couldn't forget your face because it was like I was looking in the mirror at you every day. I am confused why I didn't recognize you when I saw you."

Harvey interrupted, "I knew the Lord didn't allow either of you to see. Ami, Ahanu, and you had your eyes closed or maybe scales upon them. He wanted His timing to be perfect."

Joseph continued, "Okay, I can accept that. I was also surprised about not having the revelation about your dream. I have gotten used to hearing from Yah about the revelation of dreams almost immediately. When I first met you, I couldn't shake the feeling of knowing you. Now, I understand why. I have wanted this day to happen for so long. Now, I am in awe of how YAH orchestrated it all. Thank you, Yah! Thank you for bringing me to my mother." Joseph could hear other people crying at the reunion. He could not or would not take his eyes off his mother.

Amitola gathered herself, "I thought about you every day. I could smell you. I never lost the memory of holding you. I am so sorry I left you in that trash bin." Joseph interjected, "It's okay, mom." Amitola said, "I was so scared and ashamed. I never told anyone until I met Harvey. I was able to hide my pregnancy from everyone. I wore clothes that were too big for me. My parents thought I was going through a phase. I cried a lot, but I didn't tell my parents. They had no idea. I went through years of therapy, but no one heard my secret, only Harvey. Sometimes I felt if I didn't share the story, maybe it didn't happen. I thought I could believe I didn't give you up, but when I told Harvey my secret, I felt such a release and peace."

Joseph interrupted, "I saw my birth too, mom. I saw you on top of the building crying. I heard you tell me that you loved me." Amitola sobbed uncontrollably. She gathered herself, then continued, "I am so sorry, baby boy, that I wasn't in your life." Joseph comforted her, "It's okay. It was all in Yah's plan." Amitola gathered herself, "When I started painting you, it was as if you were there at home with me. That was extremely healing for me. I dreamt of you often at all different ages. I was always holding you and singing to you. I kissed you all over." She handed Joseph a sketch pad, "Here are some sketches I made of you as a baby." Joseph opened the sketchpad. It was full of babyfaces. Joseph said, "These do look like me." Amitola laughed, "In my dreams, you had the cutest giggles. Your smile remains the same. You look exactly as I dreamt you."

Amitola continued, "When I started to dream you. I didn't recognize that you looked just like me. God truly blinded me to that." She reached into her purse, pulled out a small pocketbook, and handed it to Joseph. "These are sketches of you, the way I saw you in my dreams." Joseph was surprised at the detail of his face, eyes, and hair. The sketches were accurate. Joseph laughed, "I guess Yah has better plans than we could ever imagine. Again, I am astonished that we didn't recognize each other."

Amitola smiled and shook her head. "I agree. After you left this morning, I kept telling Harvey that there was something so familiar about you. Of course, part of me kept saying that it was because I had dreamt about you for years." Amitola glanced at Harvey, "A couple of hours ago; I had an open vision of you when I fell. It was at that moment that YAH revealed to me who you were. Suddenly He removed the scales from my eyes, and I saw the resemblance. I began to sob uncontrollably. Harvey held me, but I couldn't verbalize what I was seeing. Finally, after quite some time, I was able to speak and tell him. He laughed and said I know. Of course, my first instinct was to be angry with him for not revealing it to me, but in his defense, God wouldn't let him." Joseph laughed, "How can you argue with that?"

Amitola laughed, "Once I was able to speak again. I immediately called your brothers. When I explained everything that had happened, they cried and laughed. By the way, they are on their way home. They want to meet their big brother." Joseph was delighted, "That is awesome! When do they arrive?" Amitola replied, "They will both arrive early tomorrow morning."

The rest of the night they spent holding each other and laughing. They shared stories of growing up and cried together. It was almost midnight when they finally realized that the other family members were getting ready to go home. Harvey and Amitola invited Joseph to come and stay with them, but Joseph gently declined. He said, "I have all my things at Ahanu's. He is truly a brother to me, but maybe I can come to stay a couple of nights this week." Amitola asked, "Will you come by in the morning on your run?" Joseph replied, "I may skip my run tomorrow and sleep in for a change. I feel exhausted from all that has happened today. I need to process and spend time with the Lord."

As they departed, Amitola felt some anxiety as if she was leaving Joseph again. She asked, "Can you text me when you arrive back at Ahanu's?" Joseph replied, "I will be happy to send you a text, mom. I will need to get used to texting and calling you, mom. I have been alone for such a long time, and now I have a family." Amitola responded, "I am so sorry; I don't mean to treat you as a child. I know you are not a small child anymore. Please forgive me." Joseph replied, "Mom, there is nothing to forgive. It is okay. I just need to get used to that."

As Joseph, Ahanu, and his family drove home, and they discussed the day's events. They were all in awe at how Creator blinded them and then released them to be able to see. They all agreed that Creator works in wondrous ways. Ahanu asked, "now what, Joseph?' Joseph responded, "I am not sure. I have three weeks off from work and no return flight home. I guess I meet my half-brothers tomorrow and then see what Yah has planned." Ahanu asked selfishly, "Will you continue to stay with us?" Joseph laughed, "If you don't mind me being around for three weeks." Meekaila replied, "No, we don't mind. I will never get tired of you being with us." Ahanu and Isabella agreed, "We love having you around. Stay as long as you like. Our home is your home." Joseph replied, "I feel that I will need a place to stay as I get used to having a mom and family. It has been a very long time since I had people that loved me and wanted to be near me."

Meekaila giggled, "Now you have so many people that love you. For the rest of your life, we will love you." Joseph softly touched Meekaila's cheek, "I love having you as my niece. You are the sweetest girl I know." As they reached the house, it was almost two in the morning. Joseph smiled, "I guess I better text mom that we have arrived home." Meekaila smiled and asked, "Have you told Lucy?" Joseph replied, "Not yet." Ahanu teased, "I think Ami has been waiting to shower you with love for such a long time. You better get ready for super mothering." Joseph admitted, "I have waited for a long time to have a family to love. Now that moment is here, and it is almost overwhelming."

Amitola texted Joseph back, 'Thank you for letting me know you made it home. Will you come by for cocoa in the morning?' Joseph replied, 'Of course, I will. What time do the boys arrive?' Amitola replied, 'Just heard from them; they both arrive at 4 am. They should be at the house about 5:30.' Joseph responded, 'If YAH wakes me up, I will be there no later than six. I am excited to meet them!' Amitola responded, 'We are all excited! See you in the morning.' Joseph texted, 'Good night, mom.' Amitola responded with hearts, 'Yoceph, sleep well, my son.'

Joseph said goodnight to Ahanu and his family, "Have a good night. I might get up early to meet my brothers. I'll text you if I end up bringing everyone over here." Ahanu replied, "We would love to host breakfast if they are interested." Joseph replied, "I will send a text and invite them. Good night Meekaila." He then headed straight to bed. Meekaila yelled from her room, "Good night, Uncle Joey!"

Joseph took a moment to message Lucy, 'I have so much to share with you. I hope we can meet up tomorrow.' Lucy replied, 'I would love that! I am free all day tomorrow.' Joseph replied, 'How about lunch? Not sure where I will be, but I will let you know.'

Joseph awoke at 5:00 am. He thought, 'Thank You YAH for my family. Today I ask for and receive an abundance of grace. YAH, You have blessed me with family. There is no one like You. You are YAH of wonders, signs, and miracles. There is no one like You. I love You, Papa. I love You, Yahushuah HaMashiach. I love You, Ruach Haqodesh! I can't wait to see what You have planned for my life and my new family.' Joseph got up and left the house.

As he arrived at Amitola and Harvey's house, he could see the lights. He walked up and rang the doorbell. He heard yelling, 'He's here!' Then, he could hear people running to the door. Benjamin opened the door and threw his arms around Joseph, "Joseph, I am so happy to meet you. I'm Benjamin." Joseph laughed, "Hi!" Then, Eli came around the corner and jumped on the two, "Joseph!" Joseph laughed, "You must be Eli." Harvey was the next to arrive, "Ben, Eli, let Joseph come into the house. Your mom is waiting to see all of you together."

The boys separated and pulled Joseph into the house. Benjamin apologized, "Sorry about the attack. Come on, let's go see mom."

As they began to sit at the kitchen table, Amitola hugged each one of them. Amitola started to cry, "You have no idea how happy I feel. Seeing all my boys together is a dream come true." Eli was the first to speak, "I can't believe how much you look like mom." Benjamin added, "Yeah, I thought I looked like her, but you look exactly like her. But manly, of course." They all laughed.

Joseph replied, "The funny thing is that Yah blinded us. We didn't see the resemblance, but I just knew I felt like I knew her." Amitola added, "I felt like you were my Yoceph but didn't want to jump to conclusions on my own. I had to have God show me." Harvey laughed, "It was weird seeing you, but I knew God had a plan. His plan was so much better than what I could have." Benjamin laughed, "We do look so much alike. It is amazing." Eli asked, "Mom said you met a relative that looks like you. Tell us all about that?" Joseph smiled, "Ahanu. When I first saw him, I thought I had a vision or something. We started talking, and one thing led to another. I invited him out to my place at Manhattan Beach, and he invited me here. He is my brother and friend. Before I forget, he would love to host everyone for breakfast today. How do you feel about that?" Benjamin smiled at Eli. Benjamin replied, "We must meet him. I think that would be awesome! Mom? Is that okay?"

Amitola replied, "I truly appreciate the offer. I was just hoping I could cook the first breakfast for the first time for all my boys." Harvey asked, "Ami, what if they join us?" Amitola's eyes lit up, "That would be great." Joseph replied, "I can send them a text. What time shall they come over?" Ami replied, "Anytime is fine. I can have breakfast ready in an hour." Joseph smiled, "Are you sure, mom?" She shook her head, "Yes. I am sure. He is the one that God used to bring you here. I want them to feel welcome to come anytime. They are all family."

Joseph sent the text, 'Hey bro. Can you come over for breakfast in an hour? You are welcome to come sooner too.' Ahanu replied immediately, 'Meekaila has been up asking if everyone was coming over or if we were going to join you. We can be there in 20 minutes.' Joseph chuckled, "Looks like they will arrive in 20 minutes." He responded, 'you remember how to get here, right?' Ahanu replied, 'Sure do. See you soon.'

Amitola asked, "Joseph, what do you like to eat for breakfast?" Joseph responded, "Anything you want to make. I love breakfast, so I can eat anything. I had menudo for the first time yesterday." Amitola laughed, "How was that experience?" Joseph chuckled, "I loved the broth, hominy, condiments, but I won't eat the tripe again." Benjamin laughed, "I remember the first time I ate menudo. I almost threw up." Amitola laughed, "You were little. You know you love the stuff now." Eli laughed and added, "Yeah, I still won't touch the stuff. I hate it when mom is cooking that stuff." Harvey shook his head, "It is an acquired taste for sure."

Amitola asked again, "So what would you like for breakfast?" Joseph asked, "Mom, I know you want to cook for me, but what if we cook for you?" Amitola was surprised, "Really?" Joseph added, "Yes. Really. I am pretty handy in the kitchen." Joseph stood up and escorted Amitola to a chair. "Come on, guys, let's fix breakfast." Eli argued, "I am not good in the kitchen." Joseph interjected, "I'll teach you. Benjamin?" Benjamin jumped up, "I would love to see mom rest. I'll help." Joseph started giving directions, "Okay. We will need flour, sugar, salt, baking powder, oil, eggs, veggies, and fruit." The boys went right to work.

Amitola and Harvey sat back and watched in amazement as the boys worked together. Joseph gave instructions, and the two younger boys followed instructions. Amitola smiled as she watched them laugh, joke, and tease each other. She was also amazed that they were immaculate as they finished mixing and preparing breakfast.

Harvey heard the doorbell and went to answer the door. He returned with Ahanu, Isabella, and Meekaila. Meekaila ran to Joseph, "Uncle Joey, your cooking smells so good." Joseph hugged her and introduced her to his brothers, "Meekaila, this is Benjamin, and this is Eli." The introductions continued. After all the introductions, Joseph added, "Breakfast will be ready in about ten minutes." He asked, "Meekaila, would you like to help us?" Meekaila asked, "May I help mommy?" Isabella answered, "Of course, you can." Eli grabbed a step stool for her and placed her next to Joseph. "Here you go, sweetheart." Joseph smiled at Meekaila, "How would you like to tell me when the pancakes are ready to be flipped?" Meekaila answered, "I would like that just fine."

They continued to share stories of their childhood. Everyone was laughing and comfortable. Joseph asked, "Isabella, did you bring some menudo?" She laughed and replied, "No, but I have a pot at home if you want some?" Meekaila giggled, "Mommy, he is just teasing you." Isabella laughed, "Yes, I know, sweetie." Joseph asked Meekaila, "So should we do buffet style or bring everything to the table?" Meekaila decided, "Buffet style I think would be best. We can put all the food on this counter." Benjamin replied, "That's a great idea. Eli and I will get it ready." Meekaila announced, "We can all grab a plate and serve ourselves, then we can say grace." Everyone followed her instructions and sat down.

Amitola asked, "Is it okay if I say grace?" Harvey smiled at his wife, "Yes, it is." Amitola began, "Father, thank You for bringing Ahanu, Isabella, and Meekaila into our lives. Thank You for giving me back my baby boy Yoceph. Thank You for making our family complete. Bless everyone at this table. May we grow closer, and may we fall in love like you intended this family to be." She paused to see if anyone would add to her prayer. Meekaila said, "Jesus come to join us today and every day." Harvey added, "Thank You, Lord, for answering our prayers." Benjamin added, "Thank You for giving me my big brother and little brother." Eli added, "I thank You for each one of my family members." Joseph added, "Papa, You have given us all so much. May we all be a blessing to others. Thank You, Papa." Joseph looked around and added, "And all Yah's saints said." Everyone said, "Amen."

As they enjoyed each other's company, it was as if they had known each other all their lives because the conversation flowed smoothly; at times, their bellies ached because of so much laughter.

Amitola was so delighted to finally have her eldest son returned to her. She smiled as she watched her boys enjoying each other. But she had to wonder about God's miracle to bring them together. She thought about every piece that God knit together to bring back her baby boy.

Joseph looked around the table. He thought to himself, 'I have always dreamt of a family like this.'

Deuteronomy 33:13-17 And of Joseph he said, "Blessed by the LORD be his land, With the precious things of heaven, with the dew, And from the deep *water* that lies beneath,
With the precious fruits of the sun, And with the precious produce of the months. "With the best things of the ancient mountains, And with the precious things of the everlasting hills, With the precious things of the earth and its fullness,
And the favor *and* goodwill of Him who dwelt in the bush.
Let *these blessings* come upon the head of Joseph, And upon the crown of the head of him who was distinguished as a prince among his brothers. "His majesty is like a firstborn young bull And his horns like the horns of the wild ox;